Precalculus

Grades 8+

by
Wayne J. Bentley

Published by Instructional Fair
an imprint of
Frank Schaffer Publications®

Instructional Fair

Author: Wayne J. Bentley
Editors: Elizabeth Flikkema, Brad Koch, John Jones
Cover Artist: Vickie Lane

Frank Schaffer Publications®

Instructional Fair is an imprint of Frank Schaffer Publications.

Send all inquiries to:
Frank Schaffer Publications
3195 Wilson Drive NW
Grand Rapids, Michigan 49534

Precalculus—grades 8+

ISBN: 1-56822-488-5

6 7 8 9 10 PAT 09 08 07

Table of Contents

Absolute Value Inequalities

> If $a > 0$, then $|x| < a$, only if $-a < x < a$
> $|x| > a$ only if $x < -a$ or $x > a$
> The conclusion of the first formula can also read $-a < x$ and $x < a$.

Example 1: $|3x - 5| < 4$ Solve for x.

Step 1: Immediately write the expression in terms of the definition.
$-4 < 3x - 5$ and $3x - 5 < 4$

Step 2: Solve the algebra. $1 < 3x$ and $3x < 9$
$$\frac{1}{3} < x \text{ and } x < 3$$

Step 3: Recombine. $\frac{1}{3} < x < 3$

Step 4: Check. Try a number from the interval in the original equation.
$|3(1) - 5| < 4, |-2| < 4, 2 < 4$. It works.

Example 2: $|3x - 5| \leq 4$ Solve for x.

Follow the steps above except "bring along" the equality sign. Answer: $\frac{1}{3} \leq x \leq 3$

Solve for x. **Note:** Multiplying or dividing by a negative number reverses the inequality.

1. $|5x - 1| < 4$

2. $|2x - 8| > 6$

3. $|5x + 10| < 7 + x$

4. $|4 - 2x| > 6$

5. $|x - 1| < x + 9$

6. $|2 - 4x| > 0$

7. $|11x| < 4 + x$

8. $|6 - 2x| > 12 + x$

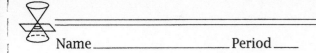

If-Then Truth Tables, Logic

Definifions
1. ~ means not
2. **p→q** means if **p**, then **q**
3. To **negate** a statement means to make a statement false if the original statement was true and vice-versa.
4. The inverse of **p→q is ~p→~q**
5. The **converse** of **p→q is q→p**
6. The **contrapositive** of **p→q** is **~q→~p**
7. The sentence p and q is true when and only when both p and q are true.
8. The sentence p or q is true in all cases except when both p and q are false.
9. The sentence p→q is true in all cases except when p is true and q is false.

Theorems
1. ~ (for all x, y) is (there exists at least one x, not y) or (there exists some x, not y)
2. ~ (there exists at least one x, y) is (for all x, not y) or (there exists some x, y) is (for all x, not y)
3. ~ (p and q) is (~p) or (~q)
4. ~ (p or q) is (~p) and (~q)
5. ~ (p → q) is p and (~q)

Example 1: Negate the following statement: All students in this class have $1.00.
Negation: At least one student in this class doesn't have $1.00.

Example 2: Negate the following statement: There exists at least one prime number greater than 10.
Negation: All prime numbers are less than or equal to 10.

Example 3: Negate the following statement: For all x, if $x^2 = a$, then $x = 3$
Negation: There exists some x such that $x^2 = 9$ and $x \neq 3$

Example 4: Write the inverse, converse, and contrapositive for the following statement: If $a > b$, then $b < a$
Inverse: If $a \leq b$, then $b \geq a$
Converse: If $b < a$, then $a > b$
Contrapositive: If $b \geq a$, then $a \leq b$

Name _____ Period ____

If-Then Truth Tables, Logic (cont.)

Example 5: Negate the following: 3 + 1 = 4 or 3 + 2 = 7
    Negation: 3 + 1 ≠ 4 and 3 + 2 ≠ 7

Example 6: Negate the following: It rained and I got wet.
    Negation: It didn't rain or I didn't get wet.

Example 7: Give the truth values for p and $\sim q$.
    a. Make up a truth table as shown and write in at first all the possibilities for p and q.

p	q	$\sim q$	p and $\sim q$
T	F		
T	T		
F	F		
F	T		

    b. Now finish filling in the table based on definitions 1, 3, and 7.

p	q	$\sim q$	p and $\sim q$
T	F	T	T
T	T	F	F
F	F	T	F
F	T	F	F

Example 8: Give the truth values for $(p \to q)$ or r.
    For the column $p \to q$, use definition 9.
    For the column $(p \to q)$ or r, use definition 8.

p	q	r	$p \to q$	$(p \to q)$ or r
T	T	T	T	T
T	T	F	T	T
T	F	T	F	T
T	F	F	F	F
F	T	T	T	T
F	T	F	T	T
F	F	T	T	F
F	F	F	T	T

Name_____ Period_____

If-Then Truth Tables, Logic (cont.)

Give the truth values for each of the following statements.

1. $p \rightarrow q$.

2. $p \rightarrow \sim q$ and r.

2. $(\sim p$ or $\sim q) \rightarrow r$.

If-Then Truth Tables, Logic (cont.)

Indirect proof:

Prove: If p, then q. Proof: Suppose $\sim q(p$ is true), and show this leads to a contradiction, therefore $\sim q$ is false and q is true.

Definitions:

n is an even integer if and only if $n = 2k$, k is an integer.

n is an odd integer if and only if $n = 2k + 1$, k is an integer.

Example 1: Prove: If $x \neq y$, then $x + 1 \neq y + 1$

Proof: Suppose $x + 1 = y + 1$, then $x = y$. This contradicts $x \neq y$ therefore $x + 1 = y + 1$ is false and $x + 1 \neq y + 1$ is true.

Example 2: Prove: If n^2 is even, then n is even.

Proof: Suppose n is odd, so $n = 2k + 1$, k is an integer. Then $n^2 = (2k + 1)^2 \quad 4k^2 + 4k + 1 = 2(2k^2 + 2k) + 1 = 2w + 1$ letting $w = 2k^2 + 2k$, thus w is an integer. Then n^2 is odd which is a contradiction. Therefore n is odd is false and n is even is true.

Note: Sometimes a statement can be proved false by a counter example.

Example 3: Prove: If $a^2 = 9$, then $a = 3$.

Proof: This is false because a could equal -3 (counter example is $a = -3$.)

Assume $x = -3$

$\quad a^2 = 9$

$\quad \therefore a^2 = 9$ and $a \neq 3$

If-Then Truth Tables, Logic (cont.)

1. Prove the if-then statements true by indirect proof or false by a counterexample.
   a. If n is an even integer, then $n^2 + 1$ is odd.

   b. If $n^2 - n$ is an even integer, then n is an odd integer.

2. Consider the premises: If you have a precalculus test the next day, then you stay up late studying. You went to bed early. What valid conclusion can you make?

   What rule did you apply?

3. Negate the following statements.
   a. All entrants are adults or are accompanied by a parent.

   b. There exists at least one real number y, where $y < 6$ and $y > 7$.

Name_____ Period____

The Inverse of a Function

The algorithm for finding the composite inverse of a function is denoted by $f^{-1}(x)$.

Example: Find the composite inverse of the function $f(x) = 3x - 2$ and check the answer.

Step 1: Replace $f(x)$ with y. $y = 3x - 2$

Step 2: Exchange x and y. $x = 3y - 2$

Step 3: Solve the equation in step 2 for y. $y = \dfrac{(x + 2)}{3} = \dfrac{x}{3} + \dfrac{2}{3}$

Step 4: Replace y with $f^{-1}(x)$. $f^{-1}(x) = \dfrac{x}{3} + \dfrac{2}{3}$

Step 5: To check the answer, take the composite of $f(x)$ and $f^{-1}(x)$.

The composite of a function and its inverse should equal x.

$f(f^{-1}(x)) = f\left(\dfrac{x}{3} + \dfrac{2}{3}\right) = 3\left(\dfrac{x}{3} + \dfrac{2}{3}\right) - 2 = x$.

Also, $f^{-1}(f(x)) = f^{-1}(3x - 2) = \dfrac{3x - 2}{3} + \dfrac{2}{3} = x$

Therefore, the inverse of $f(x) = 3x - 2$ is $f^{-1}(x) = \dfrac{x}{3} + \dfrac{2}{3}$.

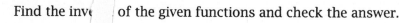

Find the inverse of the given functions and check the answer.

1. $f(x) = -x + 7$

2. $f(x) = \dfrac{1}{x} + 4$

3. $f(x) = \dfrac{-1}{(x + 1)}$

4. $f(x) = \dfrac{2x}{(x - 2)}$

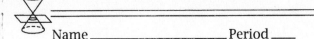

Name_____ Period____

Pascal's Triangle and Expanding a (Binomial)^n

$$
\begin{array}{ccccccccccc}
 & & & & & 1 & & & & & \\
 & & & & 1 & & 1 & & & & \\
 & & & 1 & & 2 & & 1 & & & \\
 & & 1 & & 3 & & 3 & & 1 & & \\
 & 1 & & 4 & & 6 & & 4 & & 1 & \\
1 & & 5 & & 10 & & 10 & & 5 & & 1
\end{array}
$$

$$(a + b)^0 = 1a^0b^0$$
$$(a + b)^1 = 1a + 1b$$
$$(a + b)^2 = 1a^2 + 2ab + b^2$$
$$(a + b)^3 = 1a^3 + 3a^2b + 3ab^2 + b^3$$
$$(a + b)^4 = 1a^4 + 4a^3b + 6a^2b^2 + 4ab^3 + b^4$$

Some general observations on Pascal's Triangle:

1. There is always one more term in the expansion than the power of the binomial.

2. The coefficients of the expansion are derived from Pascal's Triangle.

3. The first term in the binomial occurs in the terms of the expansion in descending powers starting with the power of the binomial and ending with zero.

4. The second term in the binomial occurs in ascending powers in the expansion starting with zero.

Example: Expand the given binomial using Pascal's Triangle.
$$(2x + y)^3$$

Step 1: Find the coefficients of the expansion from Pascal's Triangle.
$$+1 + 3 + 3 + 1$$

Step 2: Write the first term from the binomial next to the coefficients in descending powers starting with 3.
$$+1(2x)^3 + 3(2x)^2 + 3(2x) + 1(2x)^0$$

Step 3: Write the second term from the binomial behind each term in ascending powers starting with zero.
$$+1(2x)^3y^0 + 3(2x)^2y + 3(2x)y^2 + 1(2x)^0y^3$$

Step 4: In this problem, raise the 2 in each term to its respective power and multiply it by its coefficient.
$$(2x + y)^3 = 8x^3 + 12x^2y + 6xy^2 + y^3$$

Pascal's Triangle and Expanding a (Binomial)^n (cont.)

$$1$$
$$1 \quad 1$$
$$1 \quad 2 \quad 1$$
$$1 \quad 3 \quad 3 \quad 1$$
$$1 \quad 4 \quad 6 \quad 4 \quad 1$$
$$1 \quad 5 \quad 10 \quad 10 \quad 5 \quad 1$$

1. Add the next row in the coefficient pyramid for Pascal's Triangle. What is the power of the binomial it represents?

2. Expand the binomial $(x - y)^4$. **Hint:** $(x - y)^4 = (x + (-y))^4$

3. Expand the binomial $(a - 3b)^3$.

4. a. What is the leading coefficient in the expansion of the given binomial? $(5x + 2y)^6$

   b. What is the last coefficient?

   c. What is the middle coefficient?

5. Another application of Pascal's Triangle is factoring. Factor the following polynomial completely. **Hint:** factor out a constant term and look for the coefficient pattern.

$$P(x) = 7x^5 + 35x^4y + 70x^3y^2 + 70x^2y^3 + 35xy^4 + 7y^5$$

Name_____ Period_____

Complete the Square

General Form
$$y = ax^2 + bx + c$$

Standard Form
$$(y - k) = a(x - h)^2$$

Write the general equation for a parabola in standard form by completing the square.

Example: $y = 4x^2 + 8x - 6$

Step 1: Bring the constant term over to the left side of the equation. $y + 6 = 4x^2 + 8x$

Step 2: Factor out the leading coefficient. $y + 6 = 4(x^2 + 2x)$

Step 3: a. Take half the x coefficient. $\dfrac{2}{2} = 1$

        b. Square it. $(1)^2 = 1$

        c. Put it inside the parentheses. $(x^2 + 2x + 1)$

        d. Multiply it by the leading coefficient. $(4 \cdot 1 = 4)$

        e. Add the result to the left side of the equation. $y + 6 + 4 = 4(x^2 + 2x + 1)$

Step 4: What is inside the parentheses should be a perfect square. $(x^2 + 2x + 1) = (x + 1)^2$

Step 5: Simplify, and the equation is in standard form. $y + 10 = 4(x + 1)^2$

Write the general equation for a parabola in standard form by completing the square.

1. $y = 3x^2 - 9x + 5$ 2. $y = -5x^2 + 20x - 3$

3. $y = x^2 + 2 + 3$

Standard Forms for Conic Sections

General Equation
$Ax^2 + Bxy + Cy^2 + Dx + Ey + F = 0 \qquad B = 0$
Standard Forms
Parabola: $(y - k) = a(x - h)^2$ or $(x - h) = a(y - k)^2$
Ellipse: $\dfrac{(x - h)^2}{a^2} + \dfrac{(y - k)^2}{b^2} = 1$ or $\dfrac{(x - h)^2}{b^2} + \dfrac{(y - k)^2}{a^2} = 1$
Circle: $(x - h)^2 + (y - k)^2 = r^2$
Hyperbola: $\dfrac{(x - h)^2}{a^2} - \dfrac{(y - k)^2}{b^2} = 1$ or $\dfrac{(y - k)^2}{a^2} - \dfrac{(x - h)^2}{b^2} = 1$

Example: Given the general equation for conic sections, convert it to standard form.
$$25x^2 + 9y^2 + 100x - 54y - 44 = 0$$

Step 1: Group x and y terms. $(25x^2 + 100x) + (9y^2 - 54y) - 44 = 0$

Step 2: Complete the square on both x and y.
$$25(x^2 + 4x) + 9(y^2 - 6y) = 44$$
$$25(x^2 + 4x + 4) + 9(y^2 - 6y + 9) = 44 + 100 + 81$$
$$25(x + 2)^2 + 9(y - 3)^2 = 225$$

Step 3: In order to get 1 on the right side of the equation, divide the equation by 225.
$$\frac{25(x + 2)^2}{225} + \frac{9(y - 3)^2}{225} = \frac{225}{225}$$

Step 4: Reduce the fractions. $\dfrac{(x + 2)^2}{9} + \dfrac{(y - 3)^2}{25} = 1$

Given the general equation for conic sections, find the standard equation.

1. $x^2 - 4y^2 - 6x - 8y + 9 = 0$

2. $x^2 + y^2 + 8x - 6y + 21 = 0$

3. $4x^2 + 3y^2 - 24x + 30y + 99 = 0$

4. $-x^2 + 4y^2 + 2x + 2 = 0$

Name_____ Period____

Intersecting Graphs

In Calculus, students have to find the area between curves and revolve the area around an axis. In order to accomplish this task, they have to be able to find the point(s) of intersection (a precalculus activity).

Substitution Method

Example: Find the points of intersection between the line $y = 2x + 3$ and the parabola $y = x^2$.

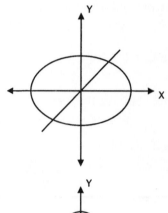

Step 1: Substitute the y-value of the line into the y-value of the parabola to obtain an equation in x.
$2x + 3 = x^2$

Step 2: Find the roots of the equation. Use factoring.

$$x^2 - 2x - 3 = 0$$
$$(x + 1)(x - 3) = 0$$
$$x = -1, x = 3$$

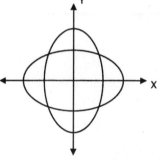

When $x = -1$, $f(x) = 1$, and when $x = 3$, $f(x) = 9$.
Therefore $(-1, 1)$ and $(3, 9)$ are the points of intersection between the line and the parabola.

Find the point(s) of intersection of the two curves.

1. $y = 3x,\quad y = -2x + 5$

2. $y = -7x,\quad y = 2x^2 + 3$

3. $y = x - 2,\quad x^2 + y^2 = 9$

4. $y = x^2,\quad y = 3x^2 - 2$

Intersecting Graphs (Conic Sections)

Substitution Method

Example: Find the points of intersection of the two conic section graphs.

$x^2 + y^2 = 4$ and $x^2 + 3y^2 - 6y = 12$

Step 1: Solve for x^2 in terms of y^2.

$x^2 = -y^2 + 4$

Step 2: Substitute for x^2 into the remaining equation.

$-y^2 + 4 + 3y^2 - 6y = 12$

Step 3: Combine and solve for y.

$2y^2 - 6y - 8 = 0$

$y^2 - 3y - 4 = 0$

$(y + 1)(y - 4) = 0$

$y = -1$ or $y = 4$. However, $y \neq 4$ because it is not part of the range of the first equation.

Step 4: Substitute -1 in for y to find the x coordinate.

$x^2 + (-1)^2 = 4$

$x^2 = 3$ and $x = +\sqrt{3}$ and $-\sqrt{3}$

Therefore the points of intersection of the two curves are $(-\sqrt{3}, -1)$ and $(\sqrt{3}, -1)$.

Find the point(s) of intersection of the two conic sections.

1. $x^2 + y^2 = 9$ and $\dfrac{x^2}{16} + \dfrac{y^2}{9} = 1$

2. $x^2 + y^2 = 16$ and $x^2 + y^2 + 4x = 11$

Name_____ Period____

Intersecting Graphs (Mixed Graphs)

Automatic Grapher Method

Sometimes there is not an easy algebraic method to find the point(s) of intersection between two curves. When this is the case, the automatic grapher can solve the problem.

Procedure: Graph both equations on the automatic grapher and then use the trace function to see where they intersect. Often this method does not give the exact value so you should check by substituting the values back in the original equation. Also, consult the calculator manual to see if there is another method to get better values for your intersections than by using the trace function.

Find the point(s) of intersection of the two curves to the nearest hundredth. Draw the graphs.

1. $y = 3^x$ and $y = x^2$

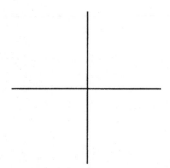

2. $y = x^2 - 3x + 4$ and $y = -x^2 + 8$

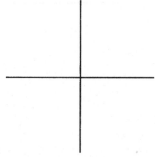

3. $f(x) = x^3 - 2$ and $f(x) = (x)^{1/2}$

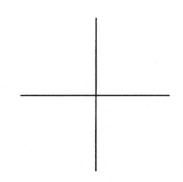

4. Find the intersection of the two curves in the first quadrant.
$y = e^x$ and $y = 2^{x-1}$

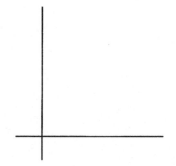

Name_____ Period____

Technological Writing: The Composite Inverse

Assignment: Technical writing is in demand in today's employment market. Your assignment is to write an analytical procedure for finding the inverse of a function. Then do a "walk through" of your procedure for finding the inverse of a function with someone that does not know what you are talking about.

Purpose: To develop analytical writing skills

Writer's Role: Develop a manual for finding the inverse of a function.

Audience: The general public

Form: Introduction to inverses (maybe use multiplicative inverse) and step by step instructions.

Focus Correction Areas:
1. Step-by-step instructions
2. Match the complexity of the procedure.
3. Try your procedure on someone.

Procedures: Use $f(x) = \dfrac{2x}{(x-3)}$ as your example.

If $P(x)$, Then $Q(x)$

Assignment: Your study partner was absent from the last class period. The teacher refuses to reteach the lesson on proving an if-then statement true by indirect proof. Your study partner says, "I don't understand the book at all. HELP!"

Purpose: Your purpose is to write out the steps so that your study partner will be able to follow them.

Writer's Role: The tutor/teacher of your study partner

Audience: Your study partner

Form: Step-by-step directions

Focus correction areas:
1. Content matches the complexity of the problem
2. Numbered steps
3. Example matches the steps

Procedure:
1. Use "If $a < b$ and $b < c$, then $a < c$."
2. You may assume that equals may be substituted for equals and $a < c$ if and only if $a + e = c$ and $e > 0$.

Name_____ Period____

Rules for Exponents

1. If the bases are the same and you are multiplying, then you add the exponents.
   Example: $(x^m)(x^n) = x^{m+n}$
   $$x^3 x^4 = x^7$$

2. If the bases are the same and you are dividing, then you subtract the exponents.
   (Also, $x^{-n} = \dfrac{1}{x^n}, x \neq 0$)
   Example: $\dfrac{x^m}{x^n} = x^{m-n}$
   $$\dfrac{x^2}{x^5} = x^{-3} = \dfrac{1}{x^3} \qquad \dfrac{x^6}{x^2} = x^4$$

3. If you have a power raised to a power, then you multiply the exponents.
   Example: $(x^m)^n = x^{mn}$
   $$(x^5)^3 = x^{15}$$

4. If you have an equation with the same base on both sides of the equal sign, then the exponents are equal.
   Example: $x^m = x^n$ then $m = n$. ($x \neq 0, 1,$ or -1)
   $$x^5 = x^m \text{ then } m = 5$$

5. If you have a product raised to a power, then each number in the product is raised to the same power.
   Example: $(xy)^m = x^m y^m$
   $$(xy)^2 = x^2 y^2$$

6. If you have a quotient raised to a power, then both the numerator and the denominator are raised to the same power.
   Example: $\left(\dfrac{x}{y}\right)^m = \dfrac{x^m}{y^m}$
   $$\left(\dfrac{x}{y}\right)^2 = \dfrac{x^2}{y^2}$$

Simplify. All exponents should be positive.

1. $\dfrac{(ab)^2 c}{a^2 b^2 c^2} =$

2. $\dfrac{b^2 (c^3)^2}{abc^4} =$

3. $\dfrac{(b^2)^4}{(b^4)^2} =$

4. $\dfrac{X^2 Y^3 Z^4}{X^4 Y^3 Z^2} =$

5. $\dfrac{Y^3 Z^3}{Z^3 Y^3} =$

6. $\dfrac{X^7 Z^6}{X^3 Y^6} =$

Name_____ Period____

Solving Exponential Equations
(Without Logarithms)

Method 1: Solving exponential equations is simplest when the bases are equal. If the bases are equal, then the exponents are equal.

Example:

$(4)^{x+2} = (4)^{2x-2}$

The bases are both 4, therefore

$x + 2 = 2x - 2$ and $x = 4$.

Check the answer. $(4)^{4+2} = (4)^{2(4)-2}$

$(4)^6 = (4)^6$

Method 2: If the bases are not equal, but they can be made equal because they are integer powers of the same base, then make the bases equal and the exponents will be equal.

Example:

$(3)^x = (27)^{5-2x}$

$27 = (3)^3$

Substitute in the new base.

$(3)^x = ((3)^3)^{5-2x}$

$(3)^x = (3)^{15-6x}$

The bases are both 3, therefore

$x = 15 - 6x$

$7x = 15$

$x = \dfrac{15}{7}$

Solve the following exponential equations.

1. $2^{2x+1} = 2^{x-3}$

2. $5^{2-2x} = 5^{x+2}$

3. $10^2 = 10^{x-4}$

4. $9^{x+7} = 3^{3-x}$

5. $16^{2x-3} = 8^x$

6. $81 = 3^{2x-4}$

Logarithm Combination Rules

$x, y,$ and $z > 0$ and $x, y,$ and z are real numbers. $b > 0, b \neq 1$.

1. The log of the product of two numbers is equal to the sum of the logs of each number.
$\log_b xy = \log_b x + \log_b y$

2. The log of the quotient of two numbers is equal to the difference of the logs of each number.
$\log_b(x/y) = \log_b x - \log_b y$

3. The log of a number raised to a power is equal to the exponent of the power multiplied by the log of the number. $\log_b x^a = a \log_b x$

4. $\log_b b = 1$

5. $\log_b 1 = 0$

Expand the logarithm.

Example:

$$\log_b\left(\frac{x^2 y}{5z^4}\right) = \log_b x^2 y - \log_b 5z^4 \quad \text{rule 2}$$

$$= \log_b x^2 + \log_b y - (\log_b 5 + \log_b z^4) \quad \text{rule 1}$$
$$= \log_b x^2 + \log_b y - \log_b 5 - \log_b z^4$$
$$= 2\log_b x + \log_b x - \log_b 5 - 4\log_b z \quad \text{rule 3}$$

1. $\log_b(3x^2 y) =$

2. $\log_b \dfrac{(abx^4 z)}{y^2} =$

3. $\log_b \dfrac{(2x^2 y z^3)}{(3x - y)} =$

Write as a single logarithm (all rules are reversible).

Example: $\log_b x - 3\log_b z + 7\log_b y - \log_b(x - 2) = \log_b x - \log_b z^3 + \log_b y^7 - \log_b(x - 2) \quad \text{rule 3}$

$$= \log_b\left(\frac{x}{z^3}\right) + \log_b\left(\frac{x^7}{x - 2}\right) \quad \text{rule 2}$$

$$= \log_b\left(\frac{xy^7}{z^3(x - 2)}\right) \quad \text{rule 1}$$

1. $3\log_b x + 5\log_b z - 2\log_b(x - 7) =$

2. $-5\log_b(x^2 + 4) + 6\log_b x - \log_b b =$

3. $2\log_b 12 - 4 + \log_b 1 =$

Hint: Write $-4\log_b b$ in place of -4.

Name_____ Period_____

Solving Simple Logarithmic Equations
Change-of-Base Rule

---

1. $\log_b x = y$ is equivalent to $b^y = x$ where $x, b > 0$ and $b \neq 1$.
2. Change-of-base rule
$$\log_b x = \frac{\log_a x}{\log_a b} \text{ where } a, b, \text{ and } x > 0 \text{ and } a, b \neq 1.$$
Note: $\log x = \log_{10} x$ and $\ln x = \log_e x$

In order to solve a simple logarithmic equation, write it as an exponential equation.

Example 1: Solve for x.

$$\log_3 x = 2$$
$$3^2 = x \qquad \text{Formula 1}$$
$$x = 9$$

Example 2: Solve for x and round to the nearest hundredth.

$$x = \log_2 5$$
$$= \frac{\log_{10} 5}{\log_{10} 2} = \frac{\log 5}{\log 2} = 2.32 \qquad \text{Formula 2}$$
$$\text{(calculator)}$$

Solve for x.

1. $\log_5 x = 2$

2. $\log_3 2x = 7$

3. $\log_4(x - 1) = 2$

4. $x = \log_2 16$

5. $x = \log_{20} 400$

6. $x = \log_{25} 625$

Solve for x using the natural log(ln) in problems 7 and 10 and round to the nearest hundredth.

7. $x = \log_2 12$

8. $3x = \log_2 32$

9. $\log_x 16 = 4$

10. $x = \log_2 e$
    Hint: $1 = \ln e$

11. $\log_{2x} 64 = 4$

Solving Exponential Equations with Logs

> If $x = y$, then
> $\log_b x = \log_b y$
> where
> b, x, and $y > 0$ and
> $b \neq 1$

Solve for x and round to the nearest thousandth.

Example 1: $\left(10^{2x}\right)^2 = 3^{x+1}$

Step 1: Simplify the exponent.
$$10^{4x} = 3^{x+1}$$

Step 2: Take the log of both sides.
$$\log 10^{4x} = \log 3^{x+1}$$

Step 3: Take the exponent out front of the log.
$$4x \log 10 = (x + 1) \log 3$$

Step 4: Use the $\log 10 = 1$ and distribute.
$$4x = x \log 3 + 1 \log 3$$

Step 5: Group the terms with an x on one side and factor out the x.
$$x(4 - \log 3) = \log 3$$

Step 6: Solve.
$$x = \frac{\log 3}{(4 - \log 3)} = .135$$

Example 2:

$$12^x = 3^{2x-1}$$
$$\log 12^x = \log 3^{2x-1}$$
$$x \log 12 = (2x - 1) \log 3$$
$$x \log 12 = 2x \log 3 - \log 3$$
$$\log 3 = 2x \log 3 - x \log 12$$
$$\log 3 = x(2 \log 3 - \log 12)$$
$$x = \frac{\log 3}{(2 \log 3 - \log 12)} = -3.189$$

1. $5^{x+2} = 10^{2x}$

2. $7^x = 10^{2x-5}$

Name_____ Period_____

Solving Exponential Equations with Logs (cont.)

Solve for x to nearest thousandth.

3. $10^x = 6^{x-2}$

4. $7^{2x} = 3^{5x-2}$

5. $5^{3x} = 8^{2x-3}$

6. $9^{2x} = 3^{-x+7}$

7. $12^x = 6^{2x-2}$

8. $11^{2x} = 102^{x-1}$

9. $e^x = 7^{2x-3}$
   Hint: Use the natural log.

10. $13^{2x} = e^{3x+1}$

Name _____ Period ___

Compound Interest

$$A = P\left(1 + \frac{r}{n}\right)^{nt}$$

A is the amount in the account after the interest is added.
P is the original principal amount in the account.
r is the yearly interest rate, expressed as a decimal, at which the account increases.
t is the length of time in years that the interest accumulates.
n is the number of times compounded annually.

Example 1: Find the amount in the account when the principal is $1000, compounded quarterly, for three years, at 6% interest.

Step 1: Identify each variable using a ? for the variable you have to find.

$A = ?$ $P = \$1000$ $r = .06$ $t = 3$ $n = 4$

Step 2: Substitute into the equation.
$$A = 1000\left(1 + \frac{.06}{4}\right)^{(.06)3}$$

Step 3: Solve the equation for the variable you need to find.
(When money, round to the nearest cent.) $A = \$1,002.68$

Example 2: How long would it take for $2,000 to double if 5% interest is compounded semi-annually?

Step 1: $A = \$4,000$ $P = \$2000$ $r = .05$ $t = ?$ $n = 2$

Step 2: $4,000 = 2,000\left(1 + \frac{.05}{2}\right)^{(2)t}$

Step 3: a. Divide both sides by 2,000 and combine the numbers inside the parentheses. $2 = (1.025)^{(2)t}$

b. Take the common log of both sides. $\log 2 = \log(1.025)^{(2)t}$

c. Using the log combination rule for exponents, bring the exponent out front.
$\log 2 = 2t \log(1.025)$

d. Therefore: $t = \log 2/(2\log(1.025))t \approx 14$ years
Note: If $\frac{r}{n}$ doesn't come out exact when dividing, then combine $1 + \frac{r}{n}$ as $\frac{n+r}{n}$ for best accuracy.

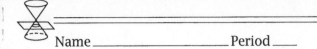

Name_____ Period____

Compound Interest (cont.)

$$A = P\left(1 + \frac{r}{n}\right)^{nt}$$

Solve for the missing variable in each problem.

Example:

$A = \$3000 \quad P = \$600 \quad r = 7\% \quad n = 4 \quad t = ?$

$$3000 = 600\left(1 + \frac{.07}{4}\right)^{4t}$$

$$5 = \left(\frac{4.07}{4}\right)^{4t}$$

$$\log 5 = \log\left(\frac{4.07}{4}\right)^{4t}$$

$$\log 5 = 4t \log\left(\frac{4.07}{4}\right)$$

$$t = \frac{\log 5}{4\log\left(\frac{4.07}{4}\right)} \approx 23.2 \text{ years}$$

1. $A = \$2000 \quad P = \$800 \quad r = 3.5\% \quad n = 12 \quad$ and $t =?$ years (nearest tenth)

2. $A = \$2500 \quad P = ? \quad r = 4.5\% \quad n = 6 \quad t = 4$ years

3. $A = ? \quad P = \$2000 \quad r = 4\% \quad n = 6 \quad t = 10$ years

4. $A = \$4000 \quad P = \$2000 \quad r = 4\% \quad n = 6 \quad t = ?$ years (nearest tenth)

Name_____ Period_____

Continuous Compound Interest

$$A = Pe^{rt}$$

A is the amount in the account after the continuous interest is added.
P is the original principal amount in the account.
r is the yearly interest rate, expressed as a decimal, at which the account increases.
t is the length of time in years that the interest is accumulated.
$e \approx 2.7182818284530$ (the shift *ln* key on a scientific calculator)

Example 1: Find the amount in the account when the principal is $1000, compounded continuously, for three years, at 6% interest.

Step 1: Identify each variable using a *?* for the variable you have to find.
   $A = ?$ $P = \$1000$ $r = .06$ $t = 3$

Step 2: Substitute into the equation.
   $A = 1000e^{(.06)3}$

Step 3: Solve the equation for the variable you have to find.
   $A = \$1197.22$

Example 2: How long would it take for $2,000 to double if 5% interest is compounded continuously? Round to the nearest tenth.

Step 1: $A = \$4,000$ $P = \$2000$ $r = .05$ $t = ?$

Step 2: $4,000 = 2,000e^{(.05)t}$

Step 3: a. Divide both sides by 2,000. $2 = e^{(.05)t}$

   b. Take the natural log of both sides. $\ln 2 = \ln e^{(.05)t}$

   c. Using the log combination rule for exponents, bring the exponent out front. $\ln 2 = .05t \ln e$

   d. Remember the $\ln e = 1$, therefore: $t = \dfrac{\ln 2}{.05}$
   $t = 13.9$ years

Name_____ Period___

Continuous Compound Interest (cont.)

$$A = Pe^{rt}$$

Solve for the missing variable in each problem.

1. $A = \$1200$ $P = \$300$ $r = ?$ $t = 4$ years (nearest hundredth percent)

2. $A = ?$ $P = \$2700$ $r = 3.5\%$ $t = 3$ years

3. $A = \$800$ $P = ?$ $r = 6\%$ $t = 10$ years

4. $A = \$1800$ $P = \$1350$ $r = 6.2\%$ $t = ?$ years (nearest hundredth)

Name _____ Period _____

Continuous Growth and Radioactive Decay

$$A = A_o e^{kt}$$

Continuous growth and radioactive decay work just like continuous compound interest. The amount of material at the end of a time frame is dependent on the amount with which you start and the rate at which it changes. The rate at which the material grows or decays, k, will be a negative value if the amount is decreasing, and positive if the amount is increasing. A_o is the original amount of material.

Example 1: At what rate is the material decaying if after 150 years 100 grams remain of a 200-gram sample?
   Note: 150 years is the half-life of the material. (Round to 4 decimal places.)

Step 1: Identify each variable. A_o = 200 grams A = 100 grams t = 150 years k = ?

Step 2: Substitute into the formula. $100 = 200e^{k150}$

Step 3: Solve for the unknown variable.

   a. Divide both sides by 200. $.5 = e^{k150}$

   b. Take the natural log of both sides. $\ln .5 = \ln e^{k150}$

   c. Using the log combination rules for exponents, bring the exponent out front.
      $= \ln .5 = (150k) \ln e$

   d. $\ln e = 1$, therefore $k = \dfrac{(\ln .5)}{150} \approx -.0046$

Example 2: At what rate is the amount of material growing if 100 bacteria in a sample increase to 250 bacteria when the sample is observed for 150 minutes? (Round to 4 decimal places.)

Step 1: Identify each variable. A_o = 100 bacteria A = 250 bacteria t = 150 minutes k = ?

Step 2: Substitute into the formula. $250 = 100e^{k150}$

Step 3: Solve for the unknown variable.

   a. Divide both sides by 100. $2.5 = e^{k150}$

   b. Take the natural log of both sides. $\ln 2.5 = \ln e^{k150}$

   c. Using the log combination rules for exponents, bring the exponent out front.
      $\ln 2.5 = (150k) \ln e$

   d. $\ln e = 1$, therefore: $k = \dfrac{(\ln 2.5)}{150} \approx .0061$

Name_____ Period_____

Continuous Growth and Radioactive Decay (cont.)

Solve for the rate of growth or decay. Round to the number of places indicated.

1. What is the rate of decay if 250 grams remain of a material that has a half-life of 2700 years? (4 decimal places)

2. What is the rate of growth of 10 bacteria if after 3.5 hours there are 2,000 bacteria? (4 decimal places)

3. How long will it take 50 grams of a substance to decay to 10 grams if the rate of decay is $k = -.345$? (nearest tenth)

4. How many bacteria will there be if 100 bacteria increase at a rate of k = 2.5/minute for 10 hours? (two significant figures)

Name_____ Period____

Radioactive Carbon Dating

Assignment: Research the process for radioactive carbon dating. Describe its uses. Develop the Mathematics. Elaborate on the assumptions necessary for radioactive dating to work.

Purpose: To elaborate on mathematics in science

Writer's Role: Field mathematician

Audience: Archeology students

Form: Report on Radioactive Carbon Dating

Focus correction areas:
1. Accuracy in research
2. Correct mathematics
3. Standard English

Procedures: The paper should reflect peer editing and include a cover page, bibliography, and foot notes.

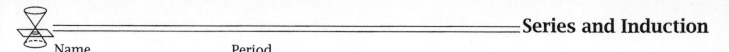

Name_____ Period____

Summation Notation and Arithmetic Series

An example of summation notation is $\displaystyle\sum_{k=2}^{5}(3k-1)$.

This is read, "The sum of $3k-1$ as k goes from 2 to 5." $\sum$ is a Greek symbol called sigma which means *sum*. k is called the index of summation. Any other letter could be used.

Example 1: In order to write $\displaystyle\sum_{k=2}^{5}(3k-1)$ in expanded form, substitute whole numbers from 2 to 5 in for k and

add as shown.

$$\sum_{k=2}^{5}(3k-1)=(3k-1)=3(2)-1+3(3)-1+3(4)-1+3(5)-1=38$$

Expand and find the sum.

1. $\displaystyle\sum_{i=4}^{8}(i)^2=$

2. $\displaystyle\sum_{p=2}^{6}3^p=$

3. $\displaystyle\sum_{t=2}^{7}10-t=$

An *arithmetic series* is an expanded sum of numbers such that each pair of consecutive numbers has a common difference. An example of this is $2+6+10+14+18+\ldots$, where the common difference is 4 $(6-2=4, 10-6=4, \text{etc.})$. To find the nth term of an arithmetic series, use the following formula: $t_n=a_1+(n-1)d$ where $t_n=n^{\text{th}}$ term, $a=$ first term, $n=$ number of terms, and $d=$ common difference. To find the 6th term of the above series, do this:

$$t_n=a_1+(n-1)d$$
$$t_6=2+(6-1)4=22$$

Now, place 22 in the series and see if it fits.

Write the following arithmetic series in summation notation ($\sum$).

Example 2: $-2+1+4+7+10+13$

Step 1: Write $\displaystyle\sum_{n=1}^{6}$ (There are 6 terms in this series; number them from 1-6)

Step 2: $t_n=a_1+(n-1)d$
$$t_n=-2+(n-1)3$$
$$=3n-5$$

So write $\displaystyle\sum_{n=1}^{6}(3n-5)$

Step 3: Check (optional)

$$\sum_{n=1}^{6}(3n-5)=3(1)-5+3(2)-5+3(3)-5+3(4)-5+3(5)-5+3(6)-5=-2+1+4+7+10+13$$

1. $3+8+13+18$

2. $(-5)+(-1)+3+7$

Geometric Series

A *geometric series* is an expanded sum of numbers (terms) such that there is a common ratio between any two consecutive terms. An example is $1 + 3 + 9 + 27 + \ldots$ where the common ratio is 3 ($\frac{3}{1} = 3, \frac{9}{3} = 3$, etc.). Use the formula $s_n = \dfrac{a_1(1 - r^n)}{1 - r}$ to find the sum of the first n terms where s_n = the sum of the first n terms, a_1 = first term, r = the common ration, and n = the number of terms.

Find the sum of the finite geometric series.

Example: $1 + \dfrac{1}{2} + \dfrac{1}{4} + \ldots + \dfrac{1}{256}$

Step 1: Notice the common ratio is $\dfrac{1}{2}$. Fill in the missing terms and see that there are 9 terms.

$$1 + \frac{1}{2} + \frac{1}{4} + \frac{1}{8} + \frac{1}{16} + \frac{1}{32} + \frac{1}{64} + \frac{1}{128} + \frac{1}{256}$$

Step 2: Use $s_n = \dfrac{a_1(1 - r^n)}{1 - r}$ $\qquad s_9 = \dfrac{1(1 - \frac{1}{2}^9)}{1 - \frac{1}{2}} = \dfrac{511}{256}$

1. $3 + 6 + 12 + 24 + 48 + \ldots + 384$

2. $\dfrac{1}{2} + \dfrac{1}{4} + \dfrac{1}{8} + \dfrac{1}{16} + \dfrac{1}{32}$

Name _____ Period _____

Geometric Series (cont.)

An infinite geometric series has a sum if and only if $|r| < 1$. Then the following formula may be used to find the sum:

$$s = \frac{a_1}{1 - r}$$

Find the sums of the infinite geometric series.

Examples:

    a. $2 + 3 + \frac{9}{2} + \frac{81}{4} + \ldots$

        $|r| = \frac{3}{2}$ and $\frac{3}{2} > 1$ so you can't find the sum.

    b. $2 + 1 + \frac{1}{2} + \frac{1}{4} + \ldots$

        $|r| = \frac{1}{2}$ so you may use the formula.

$$s = \frac{a_1}{1 - r}$$

$$= \frac{2}{1 - \frac{1}{2}}$$

$$= 4$$

1. $1 + 2 + 4 + 8 + \ldots$

2. $\frac{3}{2} + \frac{1}{2} + \frac{1}{6} + \frac{1}{18} + \ldots$

3. $-2 + \frac{2}{3} - \frac{2}{9} + \frac{2}{27} + \ldots$

Name _____ Period ____

Summation Notation Problems

Example 1: Write the following geometric series in Σ notation.

$2 + 6 + 18 + 54 + 162$

Step 1: Write $\displaystyle\sum_{n=1}^{5}$ Number the five terms in this series 1-5.

Step 2: The explicit formula to find the nth term of a geometric series is $t_n = a_1 r^{n-1}$ where $t_n = n^{\text{th}}$ term, $a_1 =$ first term, $r =$ common ration, and $n =$ number of terms.

So $t_n = a_1 r^{n-1}$

$t_n = 2(3)^{n-1}$ Now write: $\displaystyle\sum_{n=1}^{5} 2(3)^{n-1}$

Step 3: Check (optional):

$$\sum_{n=1}^{5} 2(3)^{n-1} = 2(3)^{1-1} + 2(3)^{2-1} + 2(3)^{3-1} + 2(3)^{4-1} + 2(3)^{5-1} = 2 + 6 + 18 + 54 + 162$$

The next example involves a *recursion formula* for a sequence which has rules given that. . .

    a. identify the first term or the first several terms of the sequence.

    b. state how to find subsequent terms from preceding terms.

Example 2: Generate the first four terms of the sequence from this recursive definition.

$a_1 = 3$

$a_{k+1} = a_{k-2}$

Step 1: Write $a_1 = 3$ for the first term.

Step 2: Substitute 1 for k to find the second term.

$a_{k+1} = a_k - 2$

$a_{1+1} = a_1 - 2$

$a_2 = a_1 - 2$

$a_2 = 3 - 2$ (because $a_1 = 3$)

$a_2 = 1$

Step 3: Substitute 2 and 3 for k to find the third and fourth term, respectively.

$a_{k+1} = a_k - 2$ $a_{k+1} = a_k - 2$

$a_{2+1} = a_2 - 2$ $a_{3+1} = a_3 - 2$

$a_3 = 1 - 2 = -1$ $a_4 = -1 - 2 = -3$

You should notice that a faster way to find the first four terms of this sequence is to write down the first term, 3 (because $a_1 = 3$), and keep subtracting 2 from the preceding term to get the next term (because $a_{k+1} = a_k - 2$).

Note: Be sure to keep in mind that an *explicit expression* for a sequence is a formula for each term of the sequence a_n (or t_n) in terms of n. Look at "Summation Notation and Arithmetic Series" (p 33) example 2, step 2: $t_n = 3n - 5$ is an explicit expression. You could also write this explicit expression as $a_n = 3n - 5 (t_n = a_n)$.

Also, look at example 1, step 2 above: $t_n = 2(3)^{n-1}$ or you can write $a_n = 2(3)^{n-1}$. These are explicit expressions $(a_n = t_n)$.

Name_____ Period_____

Summation Notation Problems (cont.)

Write each series in sigma notation.

1. $1 + 5 + 9 + 13 + 17 + 21$

$\sum$

2. $-3 + 6 - 12 + 24 - 48 + 96$

$\sum$

Write the terms and find the sum for the following sigma notation.

3. $\displaystyle\sum_{k=0}^{3} (k^2 - k) =$

4. $\displaystyle\sum_{i=2}^{8} (-1)^i (i^2 + 2i) =$

5. a. Generate the first five terms of the sequence from the recursive definition.
   $a_1 = 7$
   $a_{k+1} = a_k - 2$

   b. What is the explicit expression for the nth term?

Mathematical Induction Recursive Definition

Given the recursive definition for the sequence, follow the steps to prove by mathematical induction that the explicit expression for the nth term generates the terms of the sequence.

The sequence: $1, 4, 13, 40, \ldots, \dfrac{3n - 1}{2} \ldots$

The recursive definition: $a_1 = 1$
$$a_{n+1} = 3a_n + 1$$

In general, with mathematical induction we want to prove that a set S is equal to the set N of natural numbers.

Step 1: From the statement of the problem, write an equation for the nth term defined by the explicit expression.

Let $S = \left\{ n \in N : a_n = \dfrac{3^n - 1}{2} \right\}$

Step 2: Show $1 \in S$: Then take the first term of the sequence or series and set it equal to the explicit expression with 1 substituted in for n. If it turns out to be equal, then write "true $1 \in S$."

$1 = \dfrac{3^1 - 1}{2} = 1 \quad \text{true } 1 \in S$

Step 3: Assume $x \in S$: Then go back to the equation in Step 1 and substitute x for n.

$a_x = \dfrac{3x - 1}{2}$

Step 4: Prove: $x + 1 \in S$: Now go back again to the equation in Step 1 and substitute $(x + 1)$ for n.

$a_{x+1} = \dfrac{3^{x+1} - 1}{2}$

Step 5: Proof: Now go to the recursive definition and write the equation for the $x + 1$ term. Substitute into this equation the x term from the assumption, work with it algebraically until it matches the "prove" statement.

$a_{x+1} = 3a_x + 1$ (Because of the given part of the recursive definition $a_{n+1} = 3a_n + 1$, substitute x for n.)

$= 3 \left(\dfrac{3^x - 1}{2} \right) + 1$ (From Step 3: $a_x = \dfrac{3^x - 1}{2}$ and substitute $\dfrac{3x - 1}{2}$ for a_x)

$= \dfrac{3 \cdot 3^x - 3}{2} + \dfrac{2}{2}$

$= \dfrac{3^1 \cdot 3^x - 3 + 2}{2} = \dfrac{3^{x+1} - 1}{2}$

Step 6: $\therefore S = N$: Therefore, the explicit expression for the nth term generates the same sequence or series as the recursive definition.

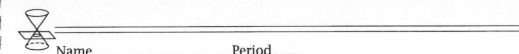
Mathematical Induction Recursive Definition (cont.)

Complete the following exercises.

1. Prove by mathematical induction that $a_n = 2^n + 1$ is the explicit expression for the nth term for the sequence defined recursively by:

$a_1 = 3$

$a_{n+1} = 2a_n - 1$

2. Prove by mathematical induction that $a_n = 5(\frac{1}{2})^{n-1}$ is the explicit expression for the nth term for the sequence defined recursively by:

$a_1 = 5$

$a_{n+1} = \dfrac{a_n}{2}$

3. Prove by mathematical induction that $a_n = \dfrac{n}{2} - \dfrac{9}{2}$ is the explicit expression for the nth term for the sequence defined recursively by:

$a_1 = -4$

$a_{n+1} = a_n + \dfrac{1}{2}$

Mathematical Induction Summation Notation

Example: Prove that $\sum_{i=1}^{n} 2i = n(n + 1)$ is true for all natural numbers.

Step 1: Write out the series equation that corresponds to the Σ.

$$\text{Let } S = \left\{ n \in N : \sum_{i=1}^{n} 2i = 2 + 4 + 6 + \ldots + 2n = n(n + 1) \right\}$$

Step 2: Show $1 \in S$: See if the first term is equal to the general formula for the sum of the first n terms of the series, substituting 1 for n. If they are equal, then write "true $1 \in S$."

$1(1 + 1) = 2 \quad$ true $1 \in S$

Step 3: Assume $x \in S$: Copy the series equation replacing n with x.

$2 + 4 + 6 + \ldots + 2x = x(x + 1)$

Step 4: Prove $x + 1 \in S$: Copy the series equation replacing n with $x + 1$. (It is important to include the last 2 terms of the series.)

$2 + 4 + 6 + \ldots + 2x + 2(x + 1) = (x + 1)[(x + 1) + 1]$

Step 5: Proof: This is the pivotal point of mathematical induction; you must find the difference between the left-hand side of the *assumption* equation and the left-hand side of the *prove* statement, then add this difference to both sides of the assumption. The difference is $2(x + 1)$.

$2 + 4 + 6 + \ldots + 2x + 2(x + 1) = x(x + 1) + 2(x + 1) \quad$ (Add $2(x + 1)$ to both sides of the assume equation in Step 3.)

$ = x^2 + x + 2x + 1$

$ = x^2 + 3x + 1$

$ = (x + 1)(x + 2)$

$ = (x + 1)[(x + 1) + 1] \quad$ (Rewrite $x + 2$ as $(x + 1) + 1$)

Step 6: Now work with the right hand side of this equation and the right hand side of the prove statement algebraically until they are identical.

Step 7: Therefore $S = N$.

Prove each statement by mathematical induction.

1. $\displaystyle\sum_{i=1}^{n} \frac{1}{i(i + 1)} = \frac{n}{(n + 1)}$

2. $\displaystyle\sum_{i=1}^{n} i^3 = \frac{[n(n + 1)]^2}{4}$

Name_____ Period____

News Demonstrates Induction

Assignment: Read an article from a national magazine such as *Newsweek* or *Time* on some current issue in national politics (welfare, health care, taxes, amendments, etc.). Look in the article for the steps of mathematical induction. Write a paragraph describing each step of mathematical induction that is demonstrated in the article: show 1 is an element of S, assume there are other examples of S, prove (we have to do something about this), proof, and therefore S is necessary for us all. How well do you feel the author proved (or disproved by counter example) his/her position?

Purpose: To recognize inductive logic

Writer's Role: To show by one example that policy in the news uses inductive logic

Audience: Journalists

Form: An essay with thesis, body, and conclusion

Focus correction areas:
1. Maintain the integrity of the article
2. Five paragraphs by order of induction
3. Clear statement of opinion as proof

Limit of a Function at a Point

$$\lim_{x \to a} F(X) = ?$$

CASE 1: If the polynomial function is defined at the point, then the limit is obtained by direct substitution.

   Example: $\lim_{x \to 2} 3x^2 - 2x + 27 = 3(2)^2 - 2(2) + 27 = 35$

CASE 2: If direct substitution results in division by zero, and the numerator is also zero, then follow the instructions for "Points of Discontinuity" (p. 45).

CASE 3: If direct substitution results in division by zero, then use your calculator to evaluate small increments close to a from both the negative and positive x directions. Note that $x = a$ is a vertical asymptote. In order for a function to have a limit at a point, its right and left hand limits have to be the same. If not, the limit does not exist.

   Example: $\lim_{x \to 3} \dfrac{x^2 - 4}{x - 3} = \dfrac{3^2 - 4}{3 - 3} = \dfrac{5}{0}$

Set up a table for x getting closer to $a = 3$ from the negative direction (from the left of 3).

x	$a = 3$
2.9	−44.1
2.99	−494.0
2.999	−4994.01

(To fill the table, do $\dfrac{2.9^2 - 4}{2.9 - 3}, \dfrac{2.99^2 - 4}{2.99 - 3}, \dfrac{2.999^2 - 4}{2.999 - 3}$)

Notice that as x gets closer to 3, $\dfrac{x^2 - 4}{x - 3}$ gets smaller without bounds, denoted as $-\infty$. Therefore, as x approaches 3 from the negative direction, the limit is $-\infty$. We write this: $\lim_{x \to 3^-} \dfrac{x^2 - 4}{x - 3} = -\infty$. You can also see this from the graph of $y = \dfrac{x^2 - 4}{x - 3}$. The darkened points show that as the x-coordinates of the points get closer to 3, the y-coordinates get smaller forever, denoted by $-\infty$. (The vertical line $x = 3$ is called an asymptote.)

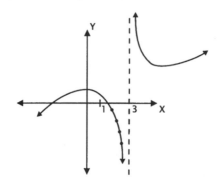

Name_____ Period_____

Limit of a Function at a Point (cont.)

Next, set up a table for x getting closer to $a = 3$ from the positive direction (from the right of 3).

x	$a = 3$
3.1	56.1
3.01	506.01
3.001	5006.001

Notice that as x gets closer to 3, $\dfrac{x^2 - 4}{x - 3}$ becomes larger without bounds, denoted by $+\infty$. Again, you can also see this from the graph of $y = \dfrac{x^2 - 4}{x - 3}$. The darkened ponts show that as the x-coordinates of the points approach 3, the y-coordinates of the points get larger forever, which we denote by $+\infty$.

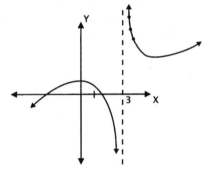

Therefore, as x gets closer to 3 from the positive direction, the limit is $+\infty$. We write:

$$\lim_{x \to 3^+} \frac{x^2 - 4}{x - 3} = +\infty$$

Find the limit of each function.

1. $\displaystyle\lim_{x \to -2} x^3 - 3x + 12 =$

2. $\displaystyle\lim_{x \to 2} \frac{x + 2}{x - 2} =$

3. $\displaystyle\lim_{x \to 3} \frac{3x^2 + 2 - 27}{x - 3} =$

4. $\displaystyle\lim_{x \to -3} \frac{x^2 + 7x + 12}{x + 3} =$

5. $\displaystyle\lim_{x \to 6} \frac{x^2 - 5x - 6}{x - 6} =$

6. $\displaystyle\lim_{x \to 1} \frac{x^3 - 1}{x^2 - 1} =$

AUTOMATIC GRAPHER: Graph number 2 to verify that $x = a$ is an asymptote.

Limits at Infinity

$$F(x) = \frac{Q(x)}{P(x)}$$

$F(x)$ is the quotient between two polynomials.

Rules for taking the limit of $f(x)$ as x approaches infinity:

1. If the degree of the numerator is equal to the degree of the denominator, then the limit is the ratio of the leading coefficients.

2. If the degree of the numerator is less than the degree of the denominator, then the limit is zero.

3. If the degree of the numerator is greater than the degree of the denominator, then the limit as a number does not exist.

Examples:

1. $\lim\limits_{x \to \infty} \dfrac{3x^3 - 2x^2 + 2x - 4}{7x^3 - 3x^2 + 2x - 27} = \dfrac{3}{7}$

The degree of the numerator (3) = degree of the denominator (3) (rule 1).

2. $\lim\limits_{x \to \infty} \dfrac{4x^2 - 2x + 27}{2x^3 - 5x + 1} = 0$

The degree of the numerator (2) < degree of the denominator (3) (rule 2).

3. $\lim\limits_{x \to \infty} \dfrac{9x^2 + 7}{x - 2}$ as a number does not exist

The degree of the numerator (2) > degree of the denominator (1) (rule 3).

Find the limit.

1. $\lim\limits_{x \to \infty} \dfrac{3x^2 - 7x + 2}{x^2 - 81} =$

2. $\lim\limits_{x \to \infty} \dfrac{-7x^3 - 2x + 27}{4x^4 - x^2 + 5} =$

3. $\lim\limits_{x \to \infty} \dfrac{-12x^2 - 24}{3x^2 - 6} =$

4. $\lim\limits_{x \to \infty} \dfrac{7x^5 - 3x^3 + 2x}{x^3 - 5x^2 + 3x} =$

5. $\lim\limits_{x \to \infty} \dfrac{x^2 - 5x^3 - 7x^4}{7x^4 - 14x^2 + 1} =$

6. $\lim\limits_{x \to \infty} \dfrac{27 - 3x^2}{3x^2 + 27} =$

AUTOMATIC GRAPHER: Use your automatic grapher to graph one from each rule to observe the behavior as the function goes to infinity

Name_____ Period____

Points of Discontinuity

$$F(x) = \frac{Q(x)}{P(x)}$$
$F(x)$ is the quotient between two polynomials.

Following is the algorithm for finding points of discontinuity.

Step 1: Given the quotient of two polynomials, take the denominator and set it equal to zero.

Step 2: Factor the equation, if possible.

Step 3: Find the value(s) of x that make the denominator zero.

Step 4: Substitute these values for x into the numerator; if any x makes the numerator zero then that value may be the x-coordinate of a point of discontinuity.

Step 5: To find the y-coordinate of the point of discontinuity, factor the numerator, cancel like factors with the denominator, then resubstitute the x value(s) from step 4. If this substitution makes the denominator 0, then there is no point of discontinuity.

Example:

$$F(x) = \frac{x^2 - 4}{x^2 - 2x - 8}$$

1. $x^2 - 2x - 8 = 0$

2. $(x + 2)(x - 4) = 0$

3. $x = -2, 4$

4. $(-2)^2 - 4 = 0, (4)^2 - 4 \neq 0$
   Therefore -2 is the x-coordinate of a point of discontinuity.

5. $\dfrac{(x - 2)(x + 2)}{(x + 2)(x - 4)} = \dfrac{(x - 2)}{(x - 4)}$, Substituting -2, $\dfrac{(-2 - 2)}{(-2 - 4)} = \dfrac{-4}{-6} = \dfrac{2}{3}$

   Therefore the point of discontinuity is $(-2, \dfrac{2}{3})$.

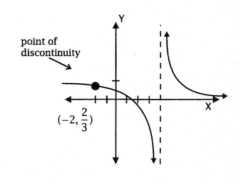

Find the point(s) of discontinuity.

1. $F(x) = \dfrac{x^2 - 1}{x^2 - 5x - 6}$

2. $F(x) = \dfrac{x^2 - 4x - 5}{x^2 - 25}$

3. $F(x) = \dfrac{x^2 + 10x + 9}{x^2 - 81}$

AUTOMATIC GRAPHER: Graph one problem, then use the trace function (or another method) to check your answer.

Name _____ Period ____

Vertical Asymptotes

$$F(x) = \frac{Q(x)}{P(x)}$$
$F(x)$ is the quotient between two polynomials.

Following is the algorithm for finding the vertical asymptotes for the graph of the quotient of two polynomials.

Step 1: Set the denominator equal to zero.

Step 2: Factor and solve for x, if possible.

Step 3: Substitute the value(s) for x into the numerator of the quotient. Those values for which the numerator is not zero are vertical asymptotes.
   Note: The values where the numerator is zero are points of discontinuity.

Find the vertical asymptotes.

Example:
$$p(x) = \frac{(2x - 2)}{(x^2 - 4)}$$

Step 1: $x^2 - 4 = 0$

Step 2: $(x - 2)(x + 2) = 0$; $x = -2$; and $x = 2$ are candidates for vertical asymptotes.

Step 3: The numerator is $2x - 2$ with $2(-2) - 2 = -6 \neq 0$ and $2(2) - 2 = 2 \neq 0$.
   Therefore the lines $x = -2$ and $x = 2$ are both vertical asymptotes.

1. $f(x) = \dfrac{x^2 - 9}{x^2 - 2x - 3}$

2. $f(x) = \dfrac{x^2 - 3x - 4}{x^2 - 16}$

3. $f(x) = \dfrac{x^2 + 7x + 6}{x^2 - 1}$

4. $f(x) = \dfrac{x^2 - 4x + 4}{x^2 - x - 2}$

5. $f(x) = \dfrac{x}{x^2 - 1}$

6. $f(x) = \dfrac{x^2 - 4}{x^2 - 9}$

7. $f(x) = \dfrac{x}{x^2 + 1}$

8. $f(x) = \dfrac{3x}{2x + 1}$

Name _____ Period ____

Horizontal and Oblique Asymptotes

$$F(x) = \frac{Q(x)}{P(x)}$$
$F(x)$ is the quotient between two polynomials.

When the limit of $f(x)$ as $|x|$ approaches infinity is zero or a constant, then y = the limit is a horizontal asymptote. $|x| \to \infty$ means $x \to \pm$

Example 1: $f(x) = \dfrac{x}{(x-1)}$

$\displaystyle\lim_{|x|\to\infty} \frac{x}{(x-1)} = 1$ Therefore $y = 1$ is an horizontal asymptote.

Example 2: $\displaystyle\lim_{|x|\to\infty} \frac{x}{(x^2-1)} = 0 \therefore y = 0$ is a horizontal asymptote.

When the limit of $f(x)$ as x approaches infinity does not exist as a number and the degree of the numerator is one more than the degree of the denominator, then the quotient of two polynomials will have an oblique asymptote.

Example 3: Find the horizontal or oblique asymptote.

$$f(x) = \frac{(x^2 - 2)}{(x-1)}$$

Step 1: Take the limit as x approaches infinity.

$\displaystyle\lim_{|x|\to\infty} \frac{(x^2-2)}{(x-1)} = \pm\infty$ (does not exist) See case 3 of "Limit of a Function at a Point" (p. 42).

Step 2: The degree of the numerator is one more than that of denominator. Therefore $f(x)$ has an oblique asymptote. To find the oblique asymptote, perform long division on the polynomials.

$$
\begin{array}{r}
x + 1\frac{-1}{(x-1)} \\[2pt]
\hline
x-1\overline{\smash{\big)}\, x^2 + 0x - 2} \\
\underline{x^2 - x} \\
0 + x - 2 \\
\underline{+ x - 1} \\
0 - 1
\end{array}
$$

Therefore, the oblique asymptote is the line $y = x + 1$.

Note: The remainder $-\dfrac{1}{x-1}$ goes to 0 as $|x| \to \infty$ so you have $x + 1$ left.

Horizontal and Oblique Asymptotes (cont.)

$$F(x) = \frac{Q(x)}{P(x)}$$
$F(x)$ is the quotient between two polynomials.

Find the horizontal or oblique asymptote.

1. $f(x) = \dfrac{(x^2 - 10x + 5)}{(3x^2 - x - 3)}$

2. $f(x) = \dfrac{(x^2 - 6x + 5)}{(x - 3)}$

3. $f(x) = \dfrac{(6x + 5)}{(10x^2 - 3x + 7)}$

4. $f(x) = \dfrac{(x^5 - 7x^2 + 5)}{(x^2 - 3x + 7)}$

5. $f(x) = \dfrac{(6x + 5)}{(x^2 - 3x + 7)}$

6. $f(x) = \dfrac{9x^2}{(3x^2 + 7)}$

7. $f(x) = \dfrac{(5x^5 - 7x^2 + 5)}{(2x^5 - 3x^4 + 2x^2 - 3x + 7)}$

8. $f(x) = \dfrac{(x^5 - 7x^2 + 5)}{(x^4 - 7x + 7)}$

Name_____ Period____

Graph the Quotient of Two Polynomials

$$F(x) = \frac{Q(x)}{P(x)}$$

$F(x)$ is the quotient between two polynomials.

Example: Graph the quotient of two polynomials.

$$f(x) = \frac{-(x-1)}{(x^2 - 10x + 9)}$$

Step 1: Find the x- and y-intercepts. To find the y-intercept, set $x = 0$ and solve. $f(0) = -\frac{1}{9}$. To find the

x-intercept(s) set y or $f(x)$ equal to zero and solve. There is no solution. The only intercept is $(0, +\frac{1}{9})$.

Step 2: To find the vertical asymptote(s) and/or point(s) of discontinuity, set the denominator equal to zero and solve.

$x^2 - 10x + 9 = 0$
$(x - 1)(x - 9) = 0, \quad x = 1$ and $x = 9$.

Because $x = 1$ makes the denominator and numerator zero, $(1, -\frac{1}{8})$ is a point of discontinuity, and $x = 9$ is a vertical asymptote.

Step 3: Take the limit of $f(x)$ as $|x|$ approaches infinity.

$$\lim_{|x| \to \infty} \frac{-(x-1)}{x^2 - 10x + 9} = 0$$

Therefore $y = 0$ is a horizontal asymptote.

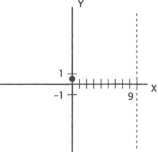

Step 4: Graph the information from steps 1, 2, and 3.

Step 5: Plot points in each region.
$x = 8, f(-3) = f(8) = 1$
$x = 10, f(10) = 1$

Step 6: Use the vertical and horizontal asymptotes, the x- and y-intercepts, the point of discontinuity, and the plotted points to sketch the graph.

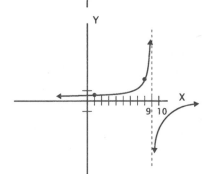

Step 7: If you have a graphing calculator, use this as a check for your graph in step 6.

Graph the Quotient of Two Polynomials (cont.)

$$F(x) = \frac{Q(x)}{P(x)}$$
$F(x)$ is the quotient between two polynomials.

Graph the quotient of two polynomials.

1. $f(x) = \dfrac{(x + 2)}{(x^2 - 8x - 9)}$

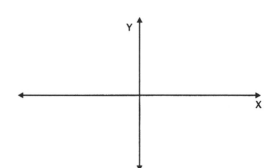

2. $f(x) = \dfrac{(x^2 - 4)}{(x^2 - 4x + 4)}$

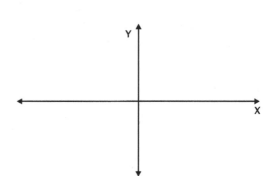

3. $f(x) = \dfrac{x^2}{(x^2 - 6x - 8)}$

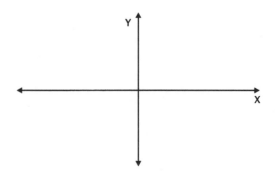

4. $f(x) = \dfrac{(x^2 - 5x + 4)}{(x - 4)}$

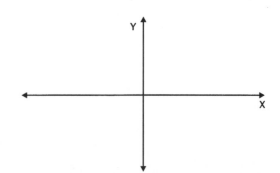

Name_____ Period____

Sum, Difference, and Product

A complex number is written $a + bi$.
Where a and b are real numbers,
a is called the *real part*, bi is
called an *imaginary number*.
($i = \sqrt{-1}$ so $i^2 = -1$).

Example: Find the sum, difference, and product for the given complex numbers.

Given $z = 5 - 3i$ and $w = 4 + 7i$

Combine the real parts and the imaginary numbers.

$$z + w = 5 - 3i + 4 + 7i = 5 + 4 - 3i + 7i$$
$$= 9 + 4i$$
$$z - w = 5 - 3i - (4 + 7i) = 5 - 3i - 4 - 7i$$
$$= 5 - 4 - 3i - 7i$$
$$= 1 - 10i$$
$$zw = (5 - 3i)(4 + 7i) = 20 + 35i - 12i - 21i^2$$
$$= 20 + 23i - 21(-1)$$
$$= 20 + 21 + 23i$$
$$= 41 + 23i$$

Find the sum, difference, and product for the given complex numbers. (For the difference, subtract the second complex number from the first.)

1. $11 - 2i$ and $3 - 4i$

2. $7 + 7i$ and $1 - i$

3. $6 + 2i$ and $5 + 5i$

4. $8 - 9i$ and $0 + 3i$

5. $27 - 13i$ and $12 + 22i$

6. $10 + \sqrt{2}i$ and $10 - \sqrt{2}i$

Name_____ Period_____

Conjugate and Quotient

> Given $z = a + bi$ and $w = c + di$
> The conjugate of the complex
> number z denoted $\bar{z}$
> $$\bar{z} = a - bi$$
> The quotient of two complex numbers
> $$\frac{a + bi}{c + di}$$

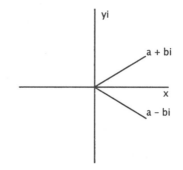

To find the quotient of two complex numbers in $a + bi$ form, multiply by one in the form of the conjugate of the numerator divided by the conjugate of the denominator and simplify.

Example: Given $z = 3 - 2i$ and $w = 4 + 5i$ find $\dfrac{z}{w}$ in complex form $(a + bi)$.

$$\frac{z}{w} = \frac{(z)(\bar{w})}{(w)(\bar{w})} = \frac{(3 - 2i)(4 - 5i)}{(4 + 5i)(4 - 5i)} = \frac{12 - 15i - 8i + 10i^2}{16 - 25i^2} = \frac{12 - 23i + 10(-1)}{16 - 25(-1)}$$

$$= \frac{2 - 23i}{41}$$

$$= \frac{2}{41} - \frac{23i}{41}$$

Find the quotient of two complex numbers in $a + bi$ form.

1. $\dfrac{3 - 3i}{6 - 6i}$

2. $\dfrac{2 + 7i}{1 + i}$

3. $\dfrac{12 - i}{2i}$

4. $\dfrac{5 + 5i}{3 + 4i}$

5. $\dfrac{22 - 11i}{7 + 7i}$

6. $\dfrac{25 + 8i}{16 - 8i}$

Name_____ Period____

Convert to Polar Form

Given the complex number $z = x + yi$

The modulus or absolute value of z written $|z| = \sqrt{x^2 + y^2}$

$\theta = \tan^{-1}(\frac{y}{x})$ for first and fourth quadrant angles

$$z = (|z|, \theta)$$

$\theta = \tan^{-1}(\frac{y}{x}) + 180°$ for second and third quadrant angles

---

The modulus of z is also called the radius of z and is the distance from the origin to the point (x, y) on the complex plane. θ is the angle that the line containing the origin and the point (x, y) makes with the positive x-axis.

Example: Convert the complex number $z = 3 + 2i$ to polar form.

Step 1: find $|z| = \sqrt{3^2 + 2^2} = \sqrt{13}$

Step 2: Find $\theta = tan^{-1}\dfrac{2}{3} = 33.7°$ (first quadrant angle)

Therefore, $z = (\sqrt{13}, 33.7°)$

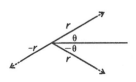

Convert the complex number to polar form (degrees to nearest tenth if rounding is necessary).

1. $3 - 7i$ 2. $7 + 6i$

3. $5 - 5i$ 4. $-6 + 3i$

5. $3 - \sqrt{2}i$ 6. $\sqrt{2} + \sqrt{2}i$

7. $\sqrt{3} - i$ 8. $-3 + 4i$

Convert Polar to Trig and $a + bi$ Forms

Given $z = (|z|, \theta)$ in polar form
Trig form of z
$z = r(\cos \theta + i \sin \theta)$
$r = |z|$
$x = r \cos \theta$ and $y = r \sin \theta$

Example: Convert the polar form of the complex number $z = (5, 45°)$ to trig form and then to $a + bi$ form.

Step 1: Substitute into the formula for trig form.
$z = 5(\cos 45° + i \sin 45°)$

Step 2: Find the $\sin 45°$ and the $\cos 45°$ and substitute.
$\sin 45° = \dfrac{\sqrt{2}}{2}$ and $\cos 45° = \dfrac{\sqrt{2}}{2}$

Step 3: Substitute into the formulas for x and y.
$x = \dfrac{5\sqrt{2}}{2}$ and $y = \dfrac{5\sqrt{2}}{2}$

Therefore, $z = 5(\cos 45° + i \sin 45°)$ in trig form and $z = \dfrac{5\sqrt{2}}{2} + \dfrac{5\sqrt{2}i}{2}$ in $a + bi$ form.

Convert the polar form of the complex number to trig form and then to $a + bi$ form. (Round to nearest hundredth.)

1. $z = (\sqrt{13}, 30°)$

2. $z = (8, 60°)$

3. $z = (10, -135°)$

4. $z = (3, 120°)$

5. $z = (35, 57°)$

6. $z = (9, 22.5°)$

Name _____ Period _____

Product and Quotient of Trig Forms

$$\text{Given } z = a(\cos\mu + i\sin\mu) \text{ and}$$
$$w = b(\cos\beta + i\sin\beta)$$
$$zw = ab(\cos(\mu + \beta) + i\sin(\mu + \beta))$$
$$\frac{z}{w} = \frac{a}{b}(\cos(\mu - \beta) + i\sin(\mu - \beta))$$

Example: Find the product and the quotient of the two complex numbers.

$z = 3(\cos 45° + i\sin 45°)$ and $w = 5(\cos 30° + i\sin 30°)$

Step 1: Substitute into the formula for the product.

$zw = (3)(5)(\cos(45° + 30°) + i\sin(45° + 30°))$

Step 2: Evaluate the formula.

$zw = 15(\cos 75° + i\sin 75°)$

Step 3: Substitute into the formula for the quotient.

$z/w = .6(\cos(45° - 30°) + i\sin(45° - 30°))$

Step 4: Evaluate the formula.

$z/w = .6(\cos 15° + i\sin 15°)$

Find the product and the quotient of the two complex numbers.

1. $7(\cos 60° + i\sin 60°)$ and $5(\cos 35° + i\sin 35°)$

2. $10(\cos 100° + i\sin 100°)$ and $.5(\cos 80° + i\sin 80°)$

3. $(\cos 30° + i\sin 30°)$ and $3(\cos 90° + i\sin 90°)$

4. $5(\cos 75° + i\sin 75°)$ and $12(\cos 45° + i\sin 45°)$

Name_____ Period____

Powers and Roots: De Moivres Theorem

Given $z = r(\cos \mu + i \sin \mu)$

$z^n = r^n(\cos n\mu + i \sin n\mu)$

$z^{1/n} = r^{1/n}\left(\cos \dfrac{(m + k360)}{n} + i \sin \dfrac{(m + k360)}{n}\right)$

$k \in \{0, 1, 2, 3, 4, \ldots, n - 1\}$

Example 1: Given $z = 3(\cos 30° + i \sin 30°)$, find z^5.

Step 1: Substitute $r = 3$, $\mu = 30°$, and $n = 5$ into the formula.

$z^5 = 3^5(\cos(5)30° + i \sin(5)30°)$

Step 2: Evaluate.

$z^5 = 243(\cos 150° + i \sin 150°)$

Example 2: Given $z^{1/5} = 32(\cos 30° + i \sin 30°)$, find the five complex roots of z.

Step 1: Substitute $r = 32$, $m = 30°$, and $n = 5$.

$z^{1/5} = 32^{1/5}\left(\cos \dfrac{(30° + k360°)}{5} + i \sin \dfrac{(30° + k360°)}{5}\right)$

Step 2: Set $k = 0$ and evaluate.

$z^{1/5} = 32^{1/5}\left(\cos \dfrac{(30° + (0)360°)}{5} + i \sin \dfrac{(30° + (0)360°)}{5}\right)$

$z^{1/5} = 2\left(\cos \dfrac{30°}{5} + i \sin \dfrac{30°}{5}\right) = 2(\cos 6° + i \sin 6°)$

Step 3: Repeat step 2 for $k = 1, 2, 3$, and 4.

$z^{1/5} = 32^{1/5}\left(\cos \dfrac{(30° + (1)360°)}{5} + i \sin \dfrac{(30° + (1)360°)}{5}\right)$

$z^{1/5} = 2(\cos 78° + i \sin 78°)$

$z^{1/5} = 32^{1/5}\left(\cos \dfrac{(30° + (2)360°)}{5} + i \sin \dfrac{(30° + (2)360°)}{5}\right)$

$z^{1/5} = 2(\cos 150° + i \sin 150°)$

$z^{1/5} = 32^{1/5}\left(\cos \dfrac{(30° + (3)360°)}{5} + i \sin \dfrac{(30° + (3)360°)}{5}\right)$

$z^{1/5} = 2(\cos 222° + i \sin 222°)$

$z^{1/5} = 32^{1/5}\left(\cos \dfrac{(30° + (4)360°)}{5} + i \sin \dfrac{(30° + (4)360°)}{5}\right)$

$z^{1/5} = 2(\cos 294° + i \sin 294°)$

1. Given $z = 6(\cos 20 + i \sin 20)$, find
   a. z^3

   b. z^6

2. Given $z = 64(\cos 48 + i \sin 48°)$, find
   a. the 3 cube roots of z.

   b. the 8 eighth roots of z.

   c. the 2 square roots of z.

       IF8768 *Precalculus*

Name_____ Period____

Analytical Roots of a Complex Number

Assignment: Develop a description of the graph of the roots of a complex number and then make an inductive generalization of the pattern and apply the generalization to two other problems. Determine if your generalization applies.

Purpose: To develop a theorem for the graphs of complex roots.

Writer's Role: Mathematician

Audience: College professors

Form: Report

Focus correction areas
1. Graphs of 3 problems
2. Step-by-step generalization
3. Correct grammar and spelling

Procedures: Use $z = 729(\cos 54° + i \sin 54°)$ With $n = 9, 6,$ or 3.

Name _____ Period ____

Triangular Trigonometry

Following are the formulas for the six trig functions in a right triangle.

$$\sin A = \frac{\text{leg opposite}}{\text{hypotenuse}} \qquad \cos A = \frac{\text{leg adjacent}}{\text{hypotenuse}} \qquad \tan A = \frac{\text{leg opposite}}{\text{leg adjacent}}$$

$$\csc A = \frac{\text{hypotenuse}}{\text{leg opposite}} \qquad \sec A = \frac{\text{hypotenuse}}{\text{leg adjacent}} \qquad \cot A = \frac{\text{leg adjacent}}{\text{leg opposite}}$$

For angle A:

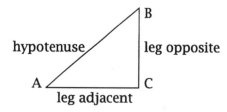

Example: Find the values of the six trig functions for angle A in the right triangle with the given measurements.

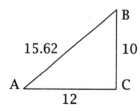

$$\sin A = \frac{10}{15.62} \qquad \cos A = \frac{12}{15.62} \qquad \tan A = \frac{10}{12}$$

$$\csc A = \frac{15.62}{10} \qquad \sec A = \frac{15.62}{12} \qquad \cot A = \frac{12}{10}$$

1. Find the values of the six trig functions for angle A in the right triangle with the given measurements.

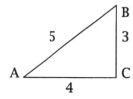

Triangular Trigonometry (cont.)

2. Find the values of the six trig functions for angle A in the right triangle with the given measurements.

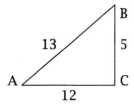

3. Find the values of the six trig functions for *angle B* in the right triangle with the given measurements.

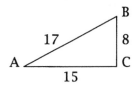

4. Find the values of the six trig functions for both angle A and angle B in the right triangle with the given measurements.

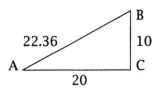

5. What do you notice about the relationships between the trig ratios for the two angles?

Inverse Trig Functions

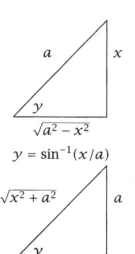

$y = \sin^{-1}(x/a)$

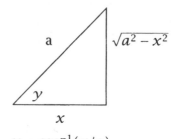

$y = \cos^{-1}(x/a)$

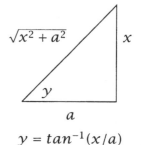

$y = tan^{-1}(x/a)$

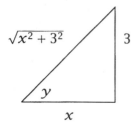

$y = cot^{-1}(x/a)$

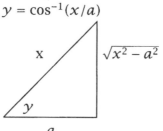

$y = \sec^{-1}(x/a)$

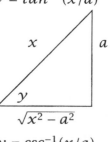

$y = \csc^{-1}(x/a)$

The formula $y = \sin^{-1} x/a$ is read in the following way: the angle whose sine is x/a (also, $\sin y = x/a$). Any inverse trig function, placed with its corresponding triangle, provides a definition of the angle y and furnishes enough information to find the other five trig functions.

Given any inverse trig function in terms of x, provide the other five trig functions (refer to p. 58).

Example: $y = \cot^{-1}(\dfrac{x}{3})$

Step 1: Draw and label the inverse cotangent triangle.

Step 2: List the six trig functions of y in terms of x.

$$\sin y = \frac{3}{\sqrt{x^2 + 3^2}}$$

$$\cos y = \frac{x}{\sqrt{x^2 + 3^2}}$$

$$\tan y = \frac{3}{x}$$

$$\cot y = \frac{x}{3}$$

$$\sec y = \frac{\sqrt{x^2 + 3^2}}{x}$$

$$\csc y = \frac{\sqrt{x^2 + 3^2}}{3}$$

Name _____ Period ____

Inverse Trig Functions (cont.)

Following are trianglular definitions of trig functions.

$$\sin y = \frac{\text{leg opposite}}{\text{hypotenuse}} \qquad\qquad \cos y = \frac{\text{leg adjacent}}{\text{hypotenuse}}$$

$$\tan y = \frac{\text{leg opposite}}{\text{leg adjacent}} \qquad\qquad \cot y = \frac{\text{leg adjacent}}{\text{leg opposite}}$$

$$\sec y = \frac{\text{hypotenuse}}{\text{leg opposite}} \qquad\qquad \csc y = \frac{\text{hypotenuse}}{\text{leg opposite}}$$

Find the six trig functions of y in terms of x.

1. $y = \dfrac{\cos^{-1} x}{2}$

2. $y = \dfrac{\csc^{-1} x}{2}$

3. $y = \dfrac{\sec^{-1} 2x}{3}$

4. $y = \dfrac{\cot^{-1} x}{8}$

5. $y = \dfrac{\sin^{-1} x}{5}$

6. $y = \tan^{-1} x$

Name _____ Period ____

Graphing Trig Functions: Sine and Cosine

$$f(x) = A\sin(Bx + C) + D$$
$$f(x) = A\cos(Bx + C) + D$$
$$D = \text{new center line}$$
$$A = \text{amplitude}$$
$$-C/B = \text{phase shift}$$
$$2\pi/B = \text{period}$$

Graph one cycle of the trig function.

Example: $f(x) = 3\sin(2x + \pi) - 1$

Step 1: Draw the new center line, $y = -1$.

Step 2: Since the amplitude is 3, draw lines $y = 2$ and $y = -4$ above and below the center line. This will eventually help you draw the curve at the correct amplitude.

Step 3: Find the phase shift. $\dfrac{-C}{B} = \dfrac{-\pi}{2}$

Draw the line $x = \dfrac{-\pi}{2}$.

Step 4: Find the period, $p = \dfrac{2\pi}{2} = \pi$. Proceed from the phase shift line a distance of π and draw a line $x = \dfrac{\pi}{2}$.

Step 5: Draw the characteristic curve.
For sin, $f(x) = \sin x$, $\sim$, (or if cosine, $f(x) = \cos x$, $\vee$). One cycle of the curve fits inside the box drawn from steps 1 through 4.

The graph of $f(x) = 3\sin(2x + \pi) - 1$

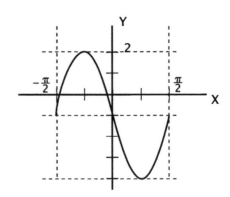

Graph one cycle of the given trig function.
$f(x) = \sin(3x - \pi) + 1$

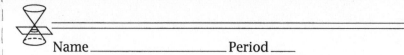

Graphing Trig Functions: Sine and Cosine (cont.)

2. $f(x) = 3 \cos\left(x - \dfrac{\pi}{2}\right) - 2$

3. $f(x) = -2 \cos\left(3x - \dfrac{\pi}{4}\right) + 2$ **Note:** A negative amplitude flips the curve.

4. $f(x) = -3 \sin(x - \pi) + 1$

5. $f(x) = \dfrac{1}{2} \sin\left(\left(\dfrac{1}{2}\right)x - \pi\right) + 2$

Trigonometry

Name_____ Period____

Graphing Trig Functions:
Tangent, Cotangent, Secant, and Cosecant

$$\tan x = \frac{\sin x}{\cos x} \qquad \sec x = \frac{1}{\cos x}$$

$$\cot x = \frac{\cos x}{\sin x} \qquad \csc x = \frac{1}{\sin x}$$

Characteristic curves:

$\tan x$ $\sec x$ $\cot x$ $\csc x$

To graph one of these four trig functions, graph the denominator, locate where the denominator is zero and draw vertical asymptotes. Determine the characteristic curve and graph between the asymptotes.

Example: Graph $f(x) = \tan(2x)$.

Step 1: Graph $f(x) = \cos(2x)$. (See p. 62.)

Step 2: Where the graph crosses the x-axis locates vertical asymptotes. Draw the vertical asymptotes.

Step 3: Draw the characteristic curve.

Graph the trig function.

1. $f(x) = \sec(3x)$

2. $f(x) = \cot(4x)$

3. $f(x) = \csc\left(\frac{x}{2}\right)$

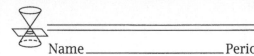

Name_____ Period____

Trig I.D. Problems

Following are some strategies for solving trig identity problems.

Step 1: Never cross over the equal sign.

Step 2: Transform the more complicated side of the identity into the simpler side.

Step 3: Transform both sides of the identity into the very same expression.

Step 4: Change functions to sines and cosines.

Step 5: Substitute using Pythagorean identities:
$$\sin^2 x + \cos^2 x = 1$$
$$1 + \tan^2 x = \sec^2 x$$
$$1 + \cot^2 x = \csc^2 x$$

Step 6: Use factoring. **Examples:**
$$\cos^2 x = 1 - \sin^2 x = (1 + \sin x)(1 - \sin x)$$
$$\tan^2 x = \sec^2 x - 1 = (\sec x - 1)(\sec x + 1)$$

Step 7: Combine terms into a single fraction.

Example: $1 + \dfrac{\cos x}{\sin x} = \dfrac{\sin x + \cos x}{\sin x}$

Step 8: Multiply by a trig value equal to 1.

Example: $\dfrac{\tan x}{1 - \cos x} = \dfrac{\tan x}{1 - \cos x} \cdot \left(\dfrac{1 + \cos x}{1 + \csc x} \right)$

Example 1: Show $\cos^2 x (1 + \cot^2 x) = \cot^2 x$

$$\cos^2 x (1 + \cot^2 x) = \cos^2 x \csc^2 x \quad \text{(Steps 2 and 4)}$$
$$= \cos^2 x \cdot \frac{1}{\sin^2 x} \quad \text{(Step 4)}$$
$$= \frac{\cos^2 x}{\sin^2 x}$$
$$= \cot^2 x$$

Example 2: Prove: $\dfrac{\tan x + \cot x}{\csc^2 x} = \tan x$

Proof: $\dfrac{\tan x + \cot x}{\csc^2 x} = \dfrac{\frac{\sin x}{\cos x} + \frac{\cos x}{\sin x}}{\frac{1}{\sin^2 x}} \quad \text{(Steps 2 and 4)}$

$$= \frac{\sin^2 x + \cos^2 x}{\cos x \sin x} \cdot \frac{\sin^2 x}{1} \quad \text{(Step 7)}$$
$$= \frac{1}{\cos x} \cdot \frac{\sin x}{1} \quad \text{(Step 5)}$$
$$= \frac{\sin x}{\cos x}$$
$$= \tan x$$

Name _____ Period ____

Trig I.D. Problems (cont.)

Example 3: Show $\tan^4 x - 1 = \sec^4 x - 2\sec^2 x$

Left side	*Right side*
$\tan^4 x - 1 = (\tan^2 x - 1)(\tan^2 x + 1)$ (Steps 3 and 6)	$\sec^4 x - 2\sec^2 x = \sec^2 x(\sec^2 x - 2)$ (Steps 3 and 5)
$\qquad = \sec^2 x(\tan^2 x - 1)$ (Step 5)	$\qquad = \sec^2 x(\tan^2 x - 2)$ (Step 5)
	$\qquad = \sec^2 x(\tan^2 x - 1)$

Example 4: Prove: $\dfrac{\cos u}{1 - \sin u} = \dfrac{1 + \sin u}{\cos u}$

$\qquad$ Proof: $\dfrac{1 + \sin u}{\cos u} = \dfrac{1 + \sin u}{\cos u}\left(\dfrac{1 - \sin u}{1 - \sin u}\right)$ (Steps 2 and 8)

$\qquad\qquad\qquad = \dfrac{1 - \sin^2 u}{\cos u(1 - \sin u)}$

$\qquad\qquad\qquad = \dfrac{\cos^2 u}{\cos u(1 - \sin u)}$ (Step 5)

$\qquad\qquad\qquad = \dfrac{\cos u}{1 - \sin u}$

Prove each identity.

1. $\dfrac{\tan^2 x}{\sec x + 1} = \sec x - 1$

2. $\dfrac{\tan x + \cot x}{\csc^2 x} = \tan x$

Name_____ Period____

Mixed Problems

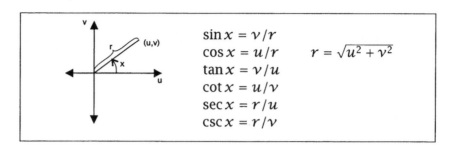

Example 1: Find the other five trig functions given $\tan x = \dfrac{-3}{2}$ and x is a fourth quadrant angle.

$$r = \sqrt{2^2 + (-3)^2} = \sqrt{13}$$

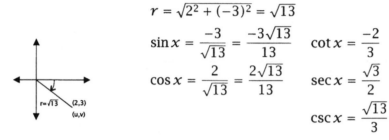

$$\sin x = \frac{-3}{\sqrt{13}} = \frac{-3\sqrt{13}}{13} \qquad \cot x = \frac{-2}{3}$$

$$\cos x = \frac{2}{\sqrt{13}} = \frac{2\sqrt{13}}{13} \qquad \sec x = \frac{\sqrt{3}}{2}$$

$$\csc x = \frac{\sqrt{13}}{3}$$

For n being an integer; general solutions
1. If $\cos x = c$, then $x = \cos^{-1} c + 360°n$ or $x = -\cos^{-1} c + 360°n$.
2. If $\sin x = c$, then $x = \sin^{-1} c + 360°n$ or $x = 180° - \sin^{-1} c + 360°n$.
3. If $\tan x = c$, then $x = \tan^{-1} c + 180°n$.

Example 2: Find the general solutions for $2\sin^2 x + 7\sin x - 4 = 0$

$2\sin^2 x + 7\sin x - 4 = 0$

$(2\sin x - 1)(\sin x + 4) = 0$

$2\sin x - 1 = 0$ or $\sin x + 4 = 0$

$\sin x = \dfrac{1}{2}$

Using 2 from above: $x = \sin^{-1}\dfrac{1}{2} + 360°n$ or $180° - \sin^{-1}\dfrac{1}{2} + 360°n$

$\qquad = 30° + 360°n$ or $150° + 360°n$

Example 3: Find the solutions for $0 \le x \le 360°$ for Example 2.

For $30° + 360°n$, let $n = 0$ and get $30°$. For $150° + 360°n$, let $n = 0$ and get $150°$.

$\therefore 30°, 150°$

Name_____ Period____

Mixed Problems (cont.)

Example 4: Use graph of $y = \cos x$ and $y = \dfrac{2}{3}$ to find the intervals between 0 and 3π where $\cos x < \dfrac{2}{3}$.

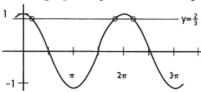

Solve $\cos x = \dfrac{2}{3}$

$x = \cos^{-1}\dfrac{2}{3} + 2\pi n$ or $-\cos^{-1}\dfrac{2}{3} + 2\pi n$ using 2 from above.

$n = 0 \qquad = \cos^{-1}\dfrac{2}{3} = .84$

$n = 1 \qquad = \cos^{-1}\dfrac{2}{3} + 2\pi = 7.12$

$n = 1 \qquad = \cos^{-1}\dfrac{2}{3} + 2\pi = 5.44$

$\therefore .84 < x < 5.44$ or $7.12 < x < 3\pi$

Sum Formulas

1. $\sin(x + y) = \sin x \cos y + \cos x \sin y$
2. $\sin(x - y) = \sin x \cos y - \cos x \sin y$
3. $\cos(x + y) = \cos x \cos y - \sin x \sin y$
4. $\cos(x - y) = \cos x \cos y + \sin x \sin y$

Example 5: Find (a) the exact value (b) an approximate value to four decimal places for $\sin\left(\dfrac{5\pi}{12}\right)$

$$\sin\left(\frac{5\pi}{12}\right) = \sin\left(\frac{3\pi}{12} + \frac{2\pi}{12}\right)$$

$$= \sin\left(\frac{\pi}{4} + \frac{\pi}{6}\right) \text{ Use formula 1 from above}$$

$$= \sin\frac{\pi}{4}\cos\frac{\pi}{6} + \frac{\cos\pi}{4}\cdot\frac{\sin\pi}{6}$$

$$= \frac{\sqrt{2}}{2}\cdot\frac{\sqrt{3}}{2} + \frac{\sqrt{2}}{2}\cdot\frac{1}{2}$$

$$= \frac{\sqrt{6}}{4} + \frac{\sqrt{2}}{4} = \frac{\sqrt{6} + \sqrt{2}}{4} \text{ exact value}$$

$$\approx .9659 \text{ appr. value}$$

Example 6: Use $\cos 2x = \cos^2 x - \sin^2 x$ in order to solve for $\cos^2 x$ in terms of $\cos 2x$.

$\cos 2x = \cos^2 x - \sin^2 x$

$\cos 2x = \cos^2 x - (1 - \cos^2 x)$ $\qquad\qquad\qquad \cos^2 x + \sin^2 x = 1$

$\cos 2x = 2\cos^2 x - 1$ $\qquad\qquad\qquad\qquad\quad \sin^2 x = 1 - \cos^2 x$

$1 + \cos 2x = 2\cos^2 x$ $\qquad\qquad\qquad\qquad\qquad$ and substitute

$\dfrac{1 + \cos 2x}{2} = \cos^2 x \qquad$ This identity is used often in calculus.

Name _____ Period ____

Mixed Problems (cont.)

1. Find the other five trig functions given $\cot x = \dfrac{4}{7}$ and x is a 3rd quadrant angle.

   a. $\sin x =$

   b. $\cos x =$

   c. $\tan x =$

   d. $\sec x =$

   e. $\csc x =$

2. Find the $\sin 2x$ when the $\sin x = .592$ and x is in the 2nd quadrant.

3. Find the general solutions to the following trig equation.
   $$5(\cos x)^2 + 4\cos x - 1 = 0$$

4. Use the graph of $y = \sin x$ and $y = \dfrac{4}{5}$ to find the intervals between 0 and 2 where $\sin x < \dfrac{4}{5}$ (use radians).

Name _____ Period _____

Mixed Problems (cont.)

1. a. Write a paragraph explaining how to solve a trig Identity.

   b. Prove the following trig identity.
      $$\tan x(\tan x + \cot x) = (\sec x)^2$$

2. a. Use special angles and sum formulas to solve the following equation.
      $$\cos\left(\frac{7\pi}{12}\right) = ?$$

   b. Check your answer with your calculator.

3. a. Use $\cos 2x = 2\cos^2 x - 1$ to solve for the $\cos x$ in terms of the $\cos 2x$.

   b. Use $\cos 2x = 1 - 2\sin^2 x$ to solve for the $\sin x$ in terms of the $\cos 2x$.

Name _____ Period _____

Mixed Problems (cont.)

Refer to a text for additional help.

1. a. Give the range and domain for $y = \sin x$ in order for the inverse sine function to be a function.

   b. Graph and label $y = \sin^{-1} x$. Also, write the domain and range for this function. How do they compare to the domain and range of $y = \sin x$?

2. a. Give the range and domain for $y = \tan x$ in order for the inverse tangent to be a function.

   b. Graph and label $y = \tan^{-1} x$ and write its domain and range. How do they compare to the domain and range of $y = \tan x$?

3. a. Give the range and domain for $y = \cos x$ in order for the inverse $\cos x$ to be a function.

   b. Graph and label $y = \cos^{-1} x$ and write its domain and range. How do they compare to the domain and range of $y = \cos x$?

Name_____ Period____

Discovering Mathematics

Assignment: Write a procedure for finding the perimeter of a triangle if the only information given is the inverse tangent function. Develop an argument for the minimum amount of additional information necessary to find the perimeter.

Purpose: Discovery, creativity, and imagination

Writer's Role: Mathematician

Audience: Precalculus students

Form: Report on procedures and findings

Focus correction areas:
1. Complexity matches the assignment
2. Correct math
3. Standard written English

Procedures: Use $y = \tan^{-1}\frac{3}{2}$. Any resource person is available to you with the exception of the teacher.

Synthetic Substitution

Synthetic substitution is used in many ways in precalculus. It is used to find the roots and evaluate, factor, and divide polynomials. These procedures would be very time consuming without synthetic substitution.

Set up:

Step 1: Bring down the coefficients.

$$f(x) = 6x^3 - 5x^2 + 7x - 8$$

Step 2: Leave a space below the coefficients and draw a line.

$$\underline{1\rfloor \quad \begin{array}{cccc} 6 & -5 & +7 & -8 \end{array}}$$
$$ 6$$

Step 3: Bring the leading coefficient below the line.

Step 4: Place the number for x that is used to evaluate $f(x)$ to the left of the coefficients (inside the symbol $\_\rfloor$).

Evaluation:

Step 5: Multiply 1 times 6 (the divisor by the first coefficient) and place it under the -5. Then add that column. Put the result, 1, under the line.

$$\begin{array}{r|rrrr} 1\rfloor & 6 & -5 & +7 & -8 \\ & & 6 & +1 & +8 \\ \hline & 6 & +1 & +8 & 0 \end{array}$$

Step 6: Repeat the process (multiply the divisor by the sum of the second column): 1 times 1 = 1. Place the result under the 7 and add. Then put the result, 8, under the line.

Step 7: Repeat the process until there are no more coefficients.

Results:

1. $f(1) = 0$ If the result is "0" then the number for x is a *root* or *zero* of the polynomial.

2. (1,0) satisfies the equation. Synthetic substitution gives us the function evaluated (the y value) at the x value.

3. The numbers in the bottom line (not including the last one) are the coeffiecients of the reduced equation. To arrive at the reduced equation, the second to the last term is the constant term, the next term is the coefficient of x^1, the next term is the coefficient of x^2, etc.
   The reduced equation:
   $6x^2 + 1x + 8$ (See also, Factor Theorem and Remainder Theorem pages.)

Note: When setting up synthetic substitution, make sure that all terms are included in the polynomial.

Example: Evaluate $p(x) = 5x^5 - 2x^3 + x - 1$ at $x = -2$

Set up:
Let $p(x) = 5x^5 + 0x^4 - 2x^3 + 0x^2 + x - 1$
$$\underline{-2\rfloor \quad \begin{array}{cccccc} 5 & +0 & -2 & +0 & +1 & -1 \end{array}}$$

Name_____ Period____

Synthetic Substitution (cont.)

1. Evaluate $f(x)$ at $x = 3$.
   $f(x) = 5x^4 - 3x^3 + 5x^2 + 0x - 10$ **Note:** 0 is the coefficient of x

2. Determine if -2 is a root of the polynomial.
   $p(x) = 3x^4 - 6x^3 + 2x^2 + 9x - 1$

3. Find the y-coordinate for the given polynomial if the x-coordinate is 2.
   $p(x) = -4x^4 - x^3 + 7x^2 + 3x - 11$

4. Find the reduced equation when the given polynomial is divided by $x = -2$.
   $p(x) = 9x^4 - 12x^3 + 17x^2 + 5x - 25$

5. Find $p(-3)$.
   $p(x) = 3x^5 - 9x^4 - 1x^3 + 12x^2 + 6x - 36$

Name _____ Period _____

Chunking: Converting to a Quadratic

$$f(x) = a(g(x))^4 + b(g(x))^2 + c = 0$$

Whenever there is an equation in the form shown above, it can be converted to a quadratic using the following procedure.

Example: Find all the values that make $f(x) = 0$.
$$f(x) = x^4 - 2x^2 - 3 = 0$$

Step 1: Label $x^2 = n$ and $(x^2)^2 = x^4 = n^2$ and substitute into $f(x)$.
$$f(x) = n^2 - 2n - 3 = 0$$

Step 2: Solve for n. In this case use factoring.
$(n + 1)(n - 3) = 0$ and $n = -1$ or $n = 3$

Step 3: Re-substitute x^2 in for n in the solutions in step 3.
$x^2 = -1$ and $x^2 = 3$.

Step 4: Solve these equations for x.
$x^2 = -1, x = \pm\sqrt{-1}, x = \pm i$
$x^2 = 3, x = \pm\sqrt{3}$
Therefore the 4 values that solve the equation are $\pm i$ and $\pm\sqrt{3}$.

Convert the equation to a quadratic and find the solutions.

1. $f(x) = x^4 - 5x^2 + 4 = 0$

2. $f(x) = 2x^4 - x^2 - 10 = 0$

3. $f(x) = 3x^4 - 8x^2 - 3 = 0$

4. $f(x) = 5x^4 - 2x^2 - 3 = 0$

Name _____ Period ____

Chunking: Converting to a Quadratic (cont.)

$$f(x) = a(g(x))^4 + b(g(x))^2 + c = 0$$

Convert the equation to a quadratic and find the solutions. Check the answers with the original equation. (Some of the solutions obtained may not satisfy the original equation.)

1. $f(x) = \sin^4 x - 5\sin^2 x + 4 = 0$

2. $f(x) = 2\cos^4 x - \cos^2 x - 10 = 0$

3. $f(x) = (\log x)^4 - 9(\log x)^2 + 8 = 0$

4. $f(x) = 5x^4 - 23x^2 - 10 = 0$

5. $f(x) = x^8 - 5x^4 - 6 = 0$

6. $f(x) = 2x^6 - 5x^3 - 12 = 0$

Name_____ Period____

Long Division of Polynomials

Long division of polynomials follows the same step as long division of rational numbers.

Example: Divide $x^4 - 4x^2 + 6x - 12$ by $x^2 - 3$

Step 1: Set up the division and put in the zero place holders.

Step 2: What must x^2 be multiplied by to give x^4? Answer x^2.

Step 3: Multiply and place in the right columns.

Step 4: Substract and bring down.

Step 5: Repeat as needed.

$$x^2 - 1 r = 6x - 15$$
$$x^2 + 0x - 3 \overline{\smash{\big)}\ x^4 + 0x^3 - 4x^2 + 6x - 12}$$
$$\underline{-(x^4 + 0x^3 - 3x^2)}$$
$$-x^2 + 6x - 12$$
$$\underline{-(-x^2 + 0x + 3)}$$
$$0 + 6x - 15$$

Perform the division.

1. Divide $3x^4 - 4x^2 + 2x - 1$ by $x^2 - 1$

2. $\dfrac{(3x^4 - 2x^3 - 4x^2 + 2x)}{(x^2 - x)}$

3. $\dfrac{(x^4 - 2x^3 + 9x^2 - 2x + 8)}{(x^2 - 2x + 8)}$

4. $\dfrac{6x^4 - 2x^3 - 10x^2 + 2x - 15}{(3x^2 - x - 4)}$

5. $\dfrac{(x^4 - 6x^3 + 6x^2 + 3x + 25)}{(x^2 - 2x + 6)}$

6. $\dfrac{-x^4 - 2x^3 - 8x^2 + 2x - 12}{(x^2 - x - 4)}$

Name _____ Period ____

$$P(x) = d(x)q(x) + r(x)$$

$p(x) = d(x)q(x) + r(x)$
$p(x)$ is any polynomial
$d(x)$ is the divisor
$q(x)$ is the quotient
$r(x)$ is the remainder

Any polynomial can be written in the form of the divisor times the quotient plus the remainder. Here are the same exercises from the preceding page (Long Division). Write them in the form of the divisor times the quotient plus the remainder.

Perform the division. Write as $p(x) = d(x)q(x) + r(x)$.

1. $p(x) = 3x^4 - 4x^2 + 2x - 1d(x) = x^2 - 1$

   Find $q(x)$ and $r(x)$.

2. $\dfrac{(3x^4 - 2x^3 - 4x^2 + 2x)}{(x^2 - x)}$

3. $\dfrac{(x^4 - 2x^3 + 9x^2 - 2x + 8)}{(x^2 - 2x + 8)}$

4. $\dfrac{6x^4 - 2x^3 - 10x^2 + 2x - 15}{(3x^2 - x - 4)}$

5. $\dfrac{(x^4 - 6x^3 + 6x^2 + 3x + 25)}{(x^2 - 2x + 6)}$

6. $\dfrac{-x^4 - 2x^3 - 8x^2 + 2x - 12}{(x^2 - x - 4)}$

Name_____ Period____

The Remainder Theorem

Consider $P(x) = d(x)q(x) + r(x)$. Suppose the divisor $d(x)$ is $x - a$, where a is a constant. Then $r(x)$ will be a constant; call it R. This is true because the divisor $x - a$ is degree 1 and the remainder has a degree 1 less than the divisor or degree 0 (or the remainder is 0), then

$$P(x) = d(x)q(x) + r(x)$$
$$P(x) = (x - a)q(x) + R$$
$$P(a) = (a - a)q(a) + R$$
$$P(a) = 0 + R$$
$$\therefore R = P(a)$$

We now have what is called the remainder theorem: $P(x) = (x - a)q(x) + P(a)$

Example: Divide the polynomial $p(x) = 3x^4 - 7x^2 + 6x - 12$ by $(x - 2)$ and express the answer in $p(x) = (x - a)q(x) + p(a)$ form.

$$\begin{array}{r|rrrrr} 2 & 3 + & 0 - & 7 + & 6 - & 12 \quad \text{note } a = 2 \text{ not } -2 \\ & & 6 & 12 & 15 & 42 \\ \hline & 3 & 6 & 5 & 21 & 30 \end{array}$$

$p(2) = 30$ and the reduced equation is $q(x) = 3x^3 + 6x^2 + 5x + 21$.
Therefore, $p(x) = (x - 2)(3x^3 + 6x^2 + 5x + 21) + 30$.

Use synthetic substitution to express the polynomial as the product of the divisor and the quotient plus the remainder.

1. $\dfrac{4x^4 - 2x^3 + 6x^2 - 5x - 19}{(x - 3)}$

2. $\dfrac{x^4 - 4x^3 + 7x^2 - 2x - 9}{(x - 1)}$

3. $\dfrac{5x^4 - x^3 + 2x^2 - 5x - 1}{(x + 2)}$

4. $\dfrac{2x^4 - 3x^3 + 7x^2 - 8x - 11}{(x + 4)}$

5. $\dfrac{1x^4 - 2x^3 + 3x^2 - 4x - 5}{(x + 10)}$

6. $\dfrac{6x^4 - 4x^3 + 2x^2 - 11}{(x + 1)}$

The Rational Root Theorem

The rational root theorem states that in a polynomial with integer coefficients, if the polynomial has any rational roots, then the root's numerator must be a factor of the constant term (c) and the root's denominator must be a factor of the leading coefficient (a).

Example: Determine all the possible rational roots for the polynomial.

$$p(x) = 3x^3 - 5x^2 + 7x - 10$$

Step 1: Determine all the factors of the constant term.
Factors of 10 are $\pm 1, \pm 2, \pm 5, \pm 10$.

Step 2: Determine all the factors of the leading coefficient.
Factors of 3 are $\pm 1, \pm 3$.

Step 3: Combine all the possibilities for the numerator and the denominator.
$\pm 1, \pm 2, \pm 5, \pm 10$ and $\pm \dfrac{1}{3}, \pm \dfrac{2}{3}, \pm \dfrac{5}{3}, \pm \dfrac{10}{3}$ are all the possible rational roots.

Determine all the possible rational roots for the polynomial.

1. $p(x) = 3x^3 - 4x^2 + 3x - 1$

2. $p(x) = x^3 - 4x^2 + 8x - 9$

3. $p(x) = 3x^3 - 4x^2 + 9x - 5$

4. $p(x) = 5x^3 - 6x^2 + 2x - 9$

Determine all the possible rational roots for the polynomial. Use synthetic substitution to determine if there are any rational roots.

5. $p(x) = 3x^3 - 7x^2 + 5x - 1$

Name_____ Period____

The Factor Theorem

The factor theorem, in general, states that when $p(r) = 0$, then r is a root of the polynomial $p(x)$, and $p(x) = (x - r)q(x)$, and the remainder is zero. $(x - r)$ is a factor of $p(x)$.

Example: Determine if $(x-3)$ is a factor of $p(x) = x^3 - 3x^2 + 6x - 18$. Express $p(x)$ as $p(x) = (x-r)q(x) + r(x)$.

$$\begin{array}{r|rrrr} 3 & 1 & -3 & +6 & -18 \\ & & 3 & 0 & 18 \\ \hline & 1 & 0 & 6 & 0 \end{array}$$

Therefore, $(x - 3)$ is a factor of $p(x) = x^3 - 3x^2 + 6x - 18$, and $r(x) = 0$.
The reduced equation is $q(x) = x^2 + 0x + 6$, $p(x) = (x - 3)(x^2 + 6)$.

Solve.

1. Determine if $(x - 2)$ is a factor of $p(x) = 2x^3 - 4x^2 + 6x - 24$. Express $p(x)$ as $p(x) = (x - r)q(x) + r(x)$.

2. Determine if 5 is a root of $p(x) = x^3 - 4x^2 + 6x - 25$. Express $p(x)$ as $p(x) = (x - r)q(x) + r(x)$.

3. Determine if 12 is a factor of $p(x) = x^3 - 32x^2 + 64x + 2112$.

The Fundamental Theorem of Algebra

The fundamental theorem of algebra, in general, states that any polynomial can be expressed as the product of prime binomials. The binomials take the form $(x - r)$ where r is a root of the polynomial. The degree of the polynomial is equal to the number of roots and binomial factors. The roots can be found over the field of complex numbers.

Some additional hints:

1. If the coefficients add to 0, then 1 is a root.

2. Change the sign on the coefficients of the odd powers of x and add them; if they add to 0, then -1 is a root.

3. The polynomial has integer coefficients. If it has any irrational roots, then the irrational roots must occur in conjugate pairs.
   Example:
   If $1 + \sqrt{2}$ is a root, then $1 - \sqrt{2}$ also has to be a root.

4. The polynomial has integer coefficients. If it has one complex root, then the complex roots must occur in conjugate pairs.
   Example:
   If $1 + i$ is a root, then $1 - i$ also has to be a root.

5. If the polynomial is an odd degree equation with integer coefficients, then there has to be at least one rational root because all other roots will occur in pairs.

Example a:
Express a fifth degree polynomial as the product of prime binomials with integer coefficients that has the roots $3, 1 + \sqrt{2}$, and i.
$$p(x) = (x - 3)(x - (1 + \sqrt{2}))(x - (1 - \sqrt{2}))(x + i)(x - i)$$

Example b:
Find the roots of the polynomial.
$$p(x) = x^5 + 3x^4 - x - 3$$

Step 1: Add the coefficients $1 + 3 - 1 - 3 = 0$; 1 is a root.

Step 2: Check if -1 is a root. Change the sign on the coefficients of the odd powers of x. Add the coefficients. $-1 + 3 + 1 - 3 = 0$; -1 is a root.

Step 3: Perform synthetic substitution with 1.

$$\begin{array}{r|rrrrrr} 1 & 1 & +3 & +0 & +0 & -1 & -3 \\ & & 1 & 4 & 4 & 4 & 3 \\ \hline \end{array}$$

Step 4: $\begin{array}{r|rrrrrr} -1 & 1 & 4 & 4 & 4 & 3 & 0 \\ & & -1 & -3 & -1 & -3 \\ \hline \end{array}$ Perform synthetic substitution with -1 on the reduced equation.

Step 5: $\begin{array}{r|rrrrr} -3 & 1 & 3 & 1 & 3 & 0 \\ & & -3 & 0 & -3 \\ \hline & 1 & 0 & 1 & 0 \end{array}$ Perform synthetic substitution with -3 (rational root theorem) on the reduced equation.

Name _____ Period ____

The Fundamental Theorem of Algebra (cont.)

Step 6: The reduced equation is $x^2 + 1 = 0$. The reduced equation, that is a quadratic, can be solved. . . .
by the quadratic formula.

$$ax^2 + bx + c = 0, \text{ then } x = \left(-b \pm \frac{\sqrt{b^2 - 4ac}}{2a}\right)$$

$$a = 1, b = 0, c = 1$$

$$x = \pm\sqrt{-4/2} = \pm i$$

by the following method.

$$x = \pm\sqrt{-1}$$

$$x^2 + 1 = 0$$

$$x^2 = -1$$

$$= \pm i$$

Therefore, the roots of the polynomial are $1, -1, -3, I - i$.

Find the roots of the polynomials.

1. $p(x) = x^3 - 7x^2 + 7x - 6$

2. $p(x) = 3x^3 + 5x^2 - 6x - 2$

3. $p(x) = x^4 + 8x^3 + 5x^2 - 8x - 6$

Algorithm for Roots of a Polynomial

Assignment: The teacher wrote a fifth degree polynomial on the overhead screen and said, "Join up with your study team and find the zeros of the polynomial over the complex field and write the polynomial as the product of prime binomial factors. Determine all the possible rational roots and the y-intercept. And determine if there are any prime quadratic factors over the real number field. Please write out the procedure."

Purpose: Match the complexity with the procedure

Writer's Role: Expert on polynomials

Audience: The study team that counts on you to know because they do their history during precalculus

Form: Analytical report

Focus correction areas:
1. Numbered steps
2. Correct mathematics
3. Standard written English

Procedures: Use $p(x) = 12x^5 - 4x^4 + 7x^3 - 2x^2 - 5x + 2 = 0$

Name_____ Period____

Rectangular to Polar Components, Standard Position, and Norm

$$\mathbf{u} = (x, y) \qquad x = r\cos\theta \qquad y = r\sin\theta \qquad \theta = \cos^{-1}\frac{x}{r} \text{ in first and second quadrants}$$

$$r = \sqrt{x^2 + y^2} \qquad |\mathbf{u}| = \sqrt{x^2 + y^2} \qquad\qquad -\cos^{-1}\frac{x}{r} \text{ in third and fourth quadrants}$$

$$\text{(norm magnitude)}$$

A vector is a quantity having magnitude and direction. It is drawn as an arrow having an initial point and an endpoint.

endpoint

initial point

An example of a vector in a real-life situation is a person walking northeast (at a 45° angle) for 2 miles.

Example: Translate the vector **u** to standard position (a vector in standard position has its initial point at the origin and it is parallel to and equal in length with the vector you are translating in the plane) convert it to polar form, and find the norm.

Parallel vectors can look like

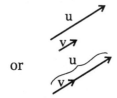

or

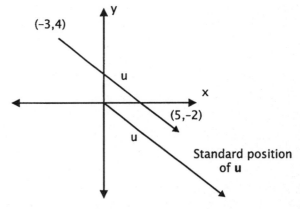

Standard position
of **u**

Step 1: To translate **u** to standard position, find the change in the x-coordinates, $5 - (-3) = 8$, and the change in the y-coordinates, $-2 - 4 = -6$.

$\mathbf{u} = (8, -6)$. Draw **u**. (For consistency, calculate endpoints coordinates minus initial points coordinates.)

Step 2: Find r. $\sqrt{8^2 + (-6)^2} = 10$

Step 3: Find θ. $\quad 8 = 10\cos\theta$

$$\frac{8}{10} = \cos\theta$$

$$\theta = -\cos^{-1}\frac{8}{10} = -36.9°$$

θ is a fourth quadrant angle, therefore $\theta = -36.9°$ and $\mathbf{u} = (10, -36.9°)$.

Step 4: Notice that the norm of the vector is equal to the radius of the vector in polar form. Find the norm.

$|u| = 10$.

Name_____ Period____

Rectangular to Polar Components, Standard Position, and Norm (cont.)

For each graph, translate the vector u to standard position, convert it to polar form, and find the norm.

1.

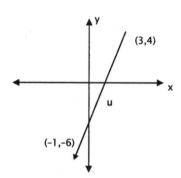

2.

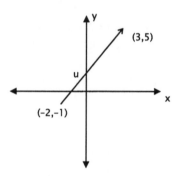

3.

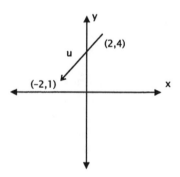

4.

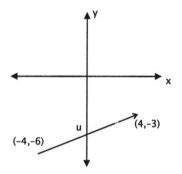

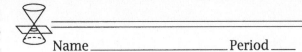

Name_____ Period____

Vector Dot Product

$\mathbf{u} = (u_1, u_2)$ and $\mathbf{v} = (v_1, v_2)$
$\mathbf{u} \cdot \mathbf{v} = u_1 v_1 + u_2 v_2$
if $\mathbf{u} \cdot \mathbf{v} = 0$, then $\mathbf{u}$ is perpendicular to $\mathbf{v}$.

Example: Find the dot product for the vectors $\mathbf{u} = (3, 4)$ and $\mathbf{v} = (-8, 6)$. Is $\mathbf{u}$ perpendicular to $\mathbf{v}$?

Step 1: Substitute into the dot product formula.
$\mathbf{u} \cdot \mathbf{v} = u_1 v_1 + u_2 v_2, \mathbf{u} \cdot \mathbf{v} = 3(-8) + 4(6) = 24 - 24 = 0$
Therefore, $\mathbf{u} \cdot \mathbf{v} = 0$ and $\mathbf{u}$ is perpendicular to $\mathbf{v}$.

Find the dot product for the vectors $\mathbf{u}$ and $\mathbf{v}$. Indicate whether $\mathbf{u}$ is perpendicular to $\mathbf{v}$.

1. $\mathbf{u} = (4, -4)$ and $\mathbf{v} = (-8, 10)$.

2. $\mathbf{u} = (7, -12)$ and $\mathbf{v} = (24, 14)$.

3. $\mathbf{u} = (27, 32)$ and $\mathbf{v} = (2, -3)$.

4. Find the dot product for the vectors $\mathbf{u}$ and $\mathbf{v}$. Indicate whether $\mathbf{u}$ is perpendicular to $\mathbf{v}$. Graph the two vectors.
$\mathbf{u} = (6, -4)$ and $\mathbf{v} = (3, -2)$.

5. Graph the two vectors. Is there any conclusion from problems 4 and 5?
$\mathbf{u} = (1, -2)$ and $\mathbf{v} = (2, -4)$.

The Angle Between Two Vectors

> $\mathbf{u} = (u_1, u_2)$ and $\mathbf{v} = (v_1, v_2)$
>
> $\mathbf{u} \cdot \mathbf{v} = u_1 v_1 + u_2 v_2$
>
> $\cos\theta = \dfrac{\mathbf{u} \cdot \mathbf{v}}{|\mathbf{u}||\mathbf{v}|}$
>
> $|\mathbf{u}| = \sqrt{(u_1)^2 + (u_2)^2}$

To find the angle between two vectors, take the dot product between the vectors and divide it by the product of their norms. Then take the inverse cosine.

Example: Find the angle between the vectors $\mathbf{u} = (3, 7)$ and $\mathbf{v} = (-2, 5)$.

Step 1: Find the dot product.
$$\mathbf{u} \cdot \mathbf{v} = 3(-2) + 7(5) = -6 + 35 = 29$$

Step 2: Find the norms of $\mathbf{u}$ and $\mathbf{v}$ and their product.
$$|\mathbf{u}| = \sqrt{(3)^2 + (7)^2} = \sqrt{58}$$
$$|\mathbf{v}| = \sqrt{(-2)^2 + (5)^2} = \sqrt{29}$$
$$|\mathbf{u}||\mathbf{v}| = \sqrt{58} \cdot \sqrt{29}$$

Step 3: Find $\dfrac{\mathbf{u} \cdot \mathbf{v}}{|\mathbf{u}||\mathbf{v}|} = \dfrac{29}{\sqrt{58} \cdot \sqrt{29}}$

Step 4: Evaluate with a calculator the inverse cosine of $\dfrac{29}{\sqrt{58} \cdot \sqrt{29}}$.

$\cos^{-1}(29/41) = 45°$

Therefore, the angle between the two vectors is $45°$.

Find the angle between the vectors (to the nearest tenth of a degree).

1. $\mathbf{u} = (6, -3)$ and $\mathbf{v} = (-2, -5)$.

2. $\mathbf{u} = (-3, -10)$ and $\mathbf{v} = (-4, 4)$.

3. $\mathbf{u} = (9, -8)$ and $\mathbf{v} = (1, -5)$.

4. $\mathbf{u} = (7, 12)$ and $\mathbf{v} = (-5, 5)$.

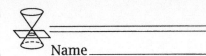

Name_____ Period____

Average Rate of Change and Average Velocity

The average rate of change from $x = a$ to $x = b$ for a function $f(x)$ is the slope of the line containing the points $(a, f(a))$ and $(b, f(b))$.

Formula for average rate of change: $\dfrac{f(b) - f(a)}{b - a}, b \neq a$.

Example: Find the average rate of change for the function $f(x) = 3x^2 - 2$ from $x = 3$ to $x = 5$.

Step 1: Find $f(5) = 3(5)^2 - 2 = 73$

Step 2: Find $f(3) = 3(3)^2 - 2 = 25$

Step 3: Evaluate formula $\dfrac{73 - 25}{5 - 3} = \dfrac{48}{2} = 24$

Therefore, 24 is the average rate of change of the function from 3 to 5.

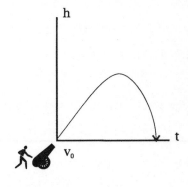

Find the average rate of change for the function given from $x = a$ to $x = b$.

1. $f(x) = -x^2 + 4 \quad a = 0 \quad b = 4$

2. $f(x) = 2/x \quad a = 1 \quad b = 5$

3. $f(x) = x^4 - 3x^2 + 4 \quad a = -1 \quad b = 2$

A special case for the average rate of change is the velocity as a function of time. Find the average velocity for the given velocity function from $t = a$ to $t = b$.

1. $v(t) = 6t^2 + 3t \quad a = 1 \quad b = 4$

2. $v(t) = 4.9t^2 + 1.6t + 10 \quad a = 1 \quad b = 10$

Name _____ Period _____

Limit Definition of the First Derivative

$$f'(x) = \lim_{h \to 0} \frac{f(x+h) - f(x)}{h}$$

The key to finding the first derivative of a function using the limit definition is to work with it algebraically until direct substitution of 0 into the formula does not result in the limit being 0/0.

Example: Using the limit definition, find the first derivative of the function $f(x) = x^2 - x + 4$.

Step 1: Find $f(x+h)$
$$f(x+h) = (x+h)^2 - (x+h) + 4$$

Step 2: Substitute into the formula for the first derivative.
$$f'(x) = \lim_{h \to 0} \frac{(x+h)^2 - (x+h) + 4 - (x^2 + x + 4)}{h}$$

Step 3: Expand the binomial raised to a power and distribute the negative.
$$f'(x) = \lim_{h \to 0} \frac{x^2 + 2hx + h^2 - x - h + 4 - x^2 + x - 4}{h}$$

Step 4: Cancel and simplify.
$$f'(x) = \lim_{h \to 0} \frac{2hx + h^2 - h}{h}$$

Step 5: Factor out the h in the numerator and cancel with the h in the denominator.
$$f'(x) = \lim_{h \to 0} \frac{h(2x + h - 1)}{h}$$

Step 6: With the cancelling of the h, direct substitution into the limit gives us the first derivative.
$$f'(x) = 2x - 1$$

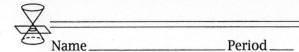

Name_____ Period____

Limit Definition of the First Derivative (cont.)

$$f'(x) = \lim_{h \to 0} \frac{f(x+h) - f(x)}{h}$$

Find the first derivative of the function using the limit definition.

1. $f(x) = x^3 - 4$

2. $f(x) = 3x^3 - 4x + 5$

3. $f(x) = 3x^2 - x + 27$

4. $f(x) = x^4 + 2x^2 - 8$

Name _____ Period _____

Instantaneous Rate of Change

$f'(x)$ evaluated at a point $x = a$.

$$f'(a) = \lim_{h \to 0} \frac{f(a + h) - f(a)}{h}$$

Example: Find the instantaneous rate of change by evaluating the first derivative at the point $x = 3$ for the function $f(x) = 3x^2 - 2x + 1$.

Step 1: Find $f(a + h)$ expand and simplify.
$f(3 + h) = 3(3 + h)^2 - 2(3 + h) + 1$
$f(3 + h) = 3(9 + 6h + h^2) - 6 - 2h + 1$
$f(3 + h) = 27 + 18h + 3h^2 - 6 - 2h + 1$
$f(3 + h) = 3h^2 + 16h + 22$

Step 2: Find $f(3)$.
$f(3) = 3(3)^2 - 2(3) + 1 = 22$

Step 3: Substitute the results from steps 1 and 2 into the formula for the limit definition of the first derivative.
$$f'(3) = \lim_{h \to 0} \frac{3h^2 + 16h + 22 - 22}{h}$$

Step 4: Simplify, factor out an h in the numerator and cancel.
$$f'(3) = \lim_{h \to 0} \frac{h(3h + 16)}{h}$$

Step 5: Evaluate the limit by direct substitution.
$f'(3) = 16$

Therefore the instantaneous rate of change of $f(x)$ at $x = 3$ is 16.

Find the instantaneous rate of change for the function at the given point.

1. $f(x) = x^3 - x$ at $x = 1$

2. $f(x) = 2x^2 - 3x$ at $x = -7$

Name_____ Period____

Instantaneous Velocity

$$f'(t) = \lim_{\Delta t \to 0} \frac{f(t + \Delta t) - f(t)}{\Delta t}$$

A special case of the instantaneous rate of change of a function (preceding page) is when the distance is expressed as a function of time(t) and the first derivative evaluated at some time $t = a$ is the instantaneous velocity. In this case we generally use Δt instead of h.

Use the steps in the example on the preceding page to find the instantaneous velocity of the function at the given time $t = a$.

1. $f(t) = 3t^2 - 4t + 8$ at $t = 2$

2. $f(t) = 4.9t^2 + 16t + 10$ at $t = 3$

3. $f(t) = 5t^2 - 4$ at $t = 10$

4. $f(t) = t^3 - 3t^2 - 1$ at $t = 3$

Algebra for the Limit Definition of the First Derivative I

$$f'(x) = \lim_{h \to 0} \frac{f(x+h) - f(x)}{h}$$

Following is the algorithm for the algebra of the first derivative of a square root function.

Step 1: Find $f(x + h)$.

Step 2: Substitute into the limit definition of the first derivative.

Step 3: Multiply the limit definition by one (1) in the form of $f(x + h) + f(x)$ divided by $f(x + h) + f(x)$.

Step 4: Simplify the numerator (do not simplify the denominator).
Cancel the h in both numerator and denominator.

Step 5: Evaluate the limit by direct substitution. The resultant formula, as a function of x, is the first derivative.

Application of Algorithm:
$f(x) = (x - 2)^{1/2}$

Step 1. $f(x + h) = ((x + h) - 2)^{1/2}$

Step 2. $f'(x) = \lim_{h \to 0} \dfrac{((x+h) - 2)^{1/2} - (x-2)^{1/2}}{h} =$

Step 3. $f'(x) = \lim_{h \to 0} \dfrac{[((x+h) - 2)^{1/2} - (x-2)^{1/2}]}{h} \dfrac{[((x+h) - 2)^{1/2} + (x-2)^{1/2}]}{[((x+h) - 2)^{1/2} + (x-2)^{1/2}]} =$

Step 4. $f'(x) = \lim_{h \to 0} \dfrac{((x+h) - 2) - (x-2)}{h[((x+h) - 2)^{1/2} + (x-2)^{1/2}]} =$

$f'(x) = \lim_{h \to 0} \dfrac{x + h - 2 - x + 2}{h[((x+h) - 2)^{1/2} + (x-2)^{1/2}]} =$

$f'(x) = \lim_{h \to 0} \dfrac{h}{h[((x+h) - 2)^{1/2} + (x-2)^{1/2}]} =$

Step 5. $f'(x) = \dfrac{1}{2(x-2)^{1/2}}$

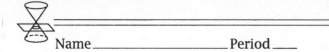

Name_____ Period____

Algebra for the Limit Definition
of the First Derivative I (cont.)

Find the first derivative of each square root function.

1. $f(x) = (x + 3)^{1/2}$

2. $f(x) = (2 - 3x)^{1/2}$

3. $f(x) = 3(x - 2)^{1/2}$

4. $f(x) = 2(1 - x)^{1/2}$

Name _____ Period ____

Algebra for the Limit Definition
of the First Derivative II

$$F'(x) = \lim_{h \to 0} \frac{f(x+h) - f(x)}{h}$$

Following is the algorithm for the algebra of the first derivative of a quotient.

Step 1: Find $f(x + h)$.

Step 2: Substitute into the limit definition of the first derivative.

Step 3: Take the common denominator in the numerator.

Step 4: Simplify the numerator and invert and cancel the h.

Step 5: Evaluate the limit by direct substitution. The resultant formula, as a function of x, is the first derivative.

Step 6. Evaluate at the value of x.

Application of Algorithm: Find the first derivative of the quotient and evaluate at the point $x = 3$. $f(x) = \dfrac{2}{x - 4}$

Step 1: $f(x + h) = \dfrac{2}{(x + h) - 4}$

Step 2: $f'(x) = \lim\limits_{h \to 0} \dfrac{\frac{2}{(x+h)-4} - \frac{2}{x-4}}{h}$

Step 3: $f'(x) = \lim\limits_{h \to 0} \dfrac{2(x-4) - 2((x+h)-4)}{\frac{((x-h)-4)(x-4)}{h}}$

Step 4: $f'(x) = \lim\limits_{h \to 0} \dfrac{2x - 8 - 2x - 2h + 8}{((x+h)-4)(x-4)} \cdot \dfrac{1}{h} = \lim\limits_{h \to 0} \dfrac{-2}{((x+h)-4)(x-4)}$

Step 5: $f'(x) = \dfrac{-2}{(x-4)^2}$

Step 6: $f'(3) = \dfrac{-2}{(3-4)^2} = -2$

Name_____ Period____

Algebra for the Limit Definition
of the First Derivative II (cont.)

$$F'(x) = \lim_{h \to 0} \frac{f(x + h) - f(x)}{h}$$

Use the limit definition of the first derivative to find $f'(x)$.

1. $f(x) = \dfrac{3}{2x - 3}$ $x = 4$

2. $f(x) = \dfrac{-1}{4 - 3x}$ $x = -2$

3. $f(x) = \dfrac{10}{2x - 6}$ $x = 5$

4. $f(x) = \dfrac{3}{x - 5}$ $x = 1$

Name_____ Period____

Tangent to the Curve at a Point

Use the limit definition of the first derivative to find the general equation, as a function of x, of the slope of the tangent line at any point. Then substitute in the given value of x and write the equation for the tangent line using point/slope form of the line.

Limit definition of the first derivative

$$f'(x) = \lim_{h \to 0} \frac{f(x+h) - f(x)}{h}$$

Point/slope form of the line $y - y_1 = m(x - x_1)$

Example: Find the tangent to the curve $f(x) = 3x^2 - 6x + 2$ at $x = 2$.
Substitute into the limit definition of the first derivative.

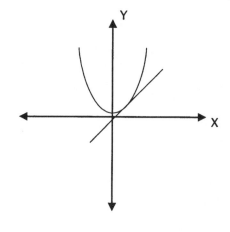

$$f'(x) = \lim_{h \to 0} \frac{3(x+h)^2 - 6(x+h) + 2 - (3x^2 - 6x + 2)}{h}$$

Expand.

$$f'(x) = \lim_{h \to 0} \frac{3x^2 + 6xh + 3h^2 - 6x - 6h + 2 - 3x^2 + 6x - 2)}{h}$$

Cancel.

$$f'(x) = \lim_{h \to 0} \frac{6xh + 3h^2 - 6h}{h}$$

Factor out the h.

$$f'(x) = \lim_{h \to 0} \frac{h(6x + 3h - 6)}{h}$$

Cancel and take the limit as h approaches 0.

$$f'(x) = \lim_{h \to 0} 6x + 3h - 6 = 6x - 6$$

Substitute 2 into $f'(x)$ to find the slope and into $f(x)$ to find the y-coordinate of the point.

$$f'(2) = 6(2) - 6 = 6$$
$$f(2) = 3(2)^2 - 6(2) + 2 = 2, x_1 = 2, \text{ and } y_1 = 2.$$

The slope $m = 6$ and the point $(x_1, y_1) = (2, 2)$. Therefore, $y - 2 = 6(x - 2)$ is the tangent to the curve at the point.

Name_____ Period____

Tangent to the Curve at a Point (cont.)

Find the tangent to the curve at the point.

1. Use $f(x) = 3x^2 - 2$ and $x = 1$.

2. Use $f(x) = \dfrac{2}{x}$ at $x = 4$.

3. Use $f(x) = (x)^{1/2}$ at $x = 9$.

4. Use $f(x) = 4x^4$ and $x = -2$.

The Power Rule or The N-Minus-One Rule

$$\text{If } f(x) = ax^n, \text{ then } f'(x) = anx^{n-1}$$

This formula is called the n-minus-one rule for finding the first derivative of a polynomial function of x.

Example 1: Use the n-minus-one rule to find the first derivative of the given function.
$f(x) = 3x^2, a = 3, n = 2$. Therefore, $f'(x) = (3)(2)x^{2-1} = 6x$.

Example 2: $f(x) = 8x$ so $f'(x) = 8$ because $8x = 8x^1$ and using the $n - 1$ rule, you get $8 \cdot 1x^{1-1} = 8x^0 = 8$

Example 3: The n-minus-one rule can be used on each term in a polynomial function to find the first derivative.
$f(x) = 5x^4 - 2x^3 - 5x^2 + 8x + 11$
$f'(x) = 20x^3 - 6x^2 - 10x + 8$. (The derivative of a constant is $= 0$ because $11 = 11x^0$, and using the $n - 1$ rule, you get $11.0x^{0-1} = 0$)

Use the n-minus-one rule to find the first derivative of the polynomial functions.

1. $f(x) = 3x^2 - 2x + 5$

2. $f(x) = 7x^7 - 3x^3 - 9$

3. $f(x) = 2x - 3x^2 - 4x^4 + 7x$

4. $f(x) = x^{-2} + x^2$

5. $f(x) = 2x^2 - 3x - 10 + 2x^{-1}$

6. $f(x) = 1/(2x)$

7. $f(x) = 10x^4 - 2x^2 + 10$

8. $f(x) = -9.8x^2 + 160x + 30$

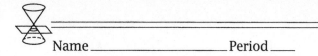

Name_____ Period_____

Horizontal Tangents, $f(x)$ Increasing or Decreasing

> If $f'(a) = 0$, then at the point $(a, f(a))$ there is a horizontal tangent
> If $f'(x) < 0$, then $f(x)$ is decreasing
> If $f'(x) > 0$, then $f(x)$ is increasing

To find the horizontal tangent(s) to a curve, use the $n - 1$ rule to obtain the first derivative. Set $f'(x) = 0$ and solve for x. The root(s) of the first derivative are where the horizontal tangent(s) occur. The function evaluated at the root(s) of the first derivative is a horizontal tangent.

Example: Find the horizontal tangent(s) to the curve. Determine the intervals on the x-axis where the function is increasing or decreasing.
$$f(x) = 2x^3 - 3x^2 - 36x + 1$$

Step 1: Use the $n - 1$ rule to find $f'(x)$.
$$f'(x) = 6x^2 - 6x - 36$$

Step 2: Set $f'(x) = 0$ and solve for x.
$6x^2 - 6x - 36 = 0$
$6(x^2 - x - 6) = 0$
$6(x - 3)(x + 2) = 0$, $x = 3$ and $x = -2$ are where the horizontal tangents occur.

Step 3: Evaluate the functions at $x = 3$ and $x = -2$.
$f(3) = 2(3)^3 - 3(3)^2 - 36(3) + 1 = -107$ and
$f(-2) = 2(-2)^3 - 3(-2)^2 - 36(-2) + 1 = 43$
Therefore, $y = -107$ and $y = 43$ are horizontal tangents.

Step 4: Determine the intervals on the x-axis where the function is increasing or decreasing. Divide the x-axis into intervals using the x values of the horizontal tangents as end points of the intervals.
$x < -2, -2 < x < 3, x > 3$

Step 5. Then evaluate $f'(x)$ at any value inside the intervals.
Choose $x = -4$. $f'(-4) = 6(-4)^2 - 6(-4) - 36 = 84, f'(x) > 0$
Choose $x = 0$. $f'(0) = -36, f'(x) < 0$
Choose $x = 4$. $f'(4) = 36, f'(x) > 0$
Therefore, $f(x)$ is increasing on $x < -2$ and $x > 3$ and $f(x)$ is decreasing on $-2 < x < 3$.

Horizontal Tangents, $f(x)$ Increasing or Decreasing (cont.)

> If $f'(a) = 0$, then at the point $(a, f(a))$ there is a horizontal tangent
> If $f'(x) < 0$, then $f(x)$ is decreasing
> If $f'(x) > 0$, then $f(x)$ is increasing

Find the horizontal tangent(s) to the curve. Determine the intervals on the x-axis where the function is increasing or decreasing.

1. $f(x) = 3x^3 - 12x^2 + 12x - 3$

2. $f(x) = x^3 - 3x^2 - 45x + 1$

3. $f(x) = 2x^3 - 39x^2 + 72x - 4$

Name_____ Period____

Using the First Derivative

1. Find the intervals for the given graph where $f'(x) > 0$, $f'(x) < 0$, and where $f'(x) = 0$.

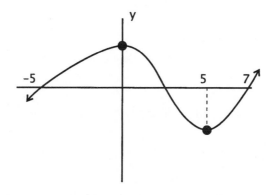

2. Find the intervals where the function increases and decreases and where all horizontal tangents occur.
   $f(x) = 3x^3 - 27x$.

3. Find all zeros of the function, the first derivative, where the horizontal tangents occur, the intervals where the function is increasing and decreasing, and find the tangent to the curve at $x = 2$.
   $f(x) = 4x^3 + 3x^2 - 90x + 83$

Name_____ Period____

Using the First Derivative (cont.)

1. Use Pascal's triangle to expand $(x + h)^3$.

2. Use the results of the previous problem to find the general formula for the first derivative of the given function using the limit definition.

$f(x) = x^3 - 2x + 4$

3. a. Find the general formula for the instantaneous rate of change for the given quadratic.

$f(x) = 8x^2 - 2x + 8$

b. What is the slope of the tangent line at $x = -2$?

4. a. Find the general formulas for the instantaneous velocity and acceleration from the given displacement formula. (The derivative of the instantaneous velocity formula will give you the instantaneous acceleration formula.)

$s(t) = -3t^2 + 5t + 10$

b. Evaluate both at $t = 5$.

Name _____ Period ____

Using the First Derivative (cont.)

Find the average rate of change for each of the given functions.

1. $f(x) = 3x^2 - 2x + 10$ from $x = 3$ to $x = 12$.

2. $f(x) = \dfrac{1}{x}$ from $x = -10$ to $x = -2$.

Find the average velocity for each of the given functions.

3. $f(x) = \sin 2x$ from $x = \dfrac{\pi}{2}$ to $x = \dfrac{5\pi}{6}$.

4. $f(x) = -2x^2 + 3x - 7$ from $x = 2$ to $x = 6$.

Find the general formula for the instantaneous rate of change for the given function.

5. $f(x) = \dfrac{2}{3x}$

6. Find the slope of the curve at $x = 2$.

Name _____ Period ____

The Final Problem

Find the roots of the polynomial, the y-intercept, the first derivative, the horizontal tangents, and the intervals on the x-axis where the function is increasing and decreasing. Express the polynomial as the product of prime binomial factors, the tangent to the polynomial curve at a point where $x = y$, and determine the intervals on the x-axis where the polynomial is positive and negative.

$p(x) = 4x^3 + 4x^2 - 32x + 24$ at $x = 5$

roots:

y-intercept:

$p'(x) =$

horizontal tangents:

$p(x)$ increasing:

$p(x)$ decreasing:

$p(x) = (x\ \ )(x\ \ (\ \ ))(\ \ (\ \ ))$

tangent at $x = 5$:

$p(x) > 0$:

$p(x) < 0$:

In calculus, you will add to these the second derivative, points of inflection, intervals where the function is concave up or concave down, the area between the curve and the x-axis, the linear approximation at a point, and the anti-derivative.

Answer Key

Page 4.

1. $-4 < 5x - 1$ and $5x - 1 < 4$

   $-3 < 5x$ $5x < 5$

   $\dfrac{-3}{5} < x$ $x < \dfrac{5}{5}$

   $x > \dfrac{-3}{5}$ and $x < 1$

                       $\dfrac{-3}{5} < x < 1$

2. $2x - 8 \le -6$ or $2x - 8 \ge 6$

   $2x \le 2$ $2x \ge 14$

   $x \le 1$ or $x \ge 7$

3. $-(7 + x) < 5x + 10$ and $5x + 10 < 7 + x$

   $-17 < 6x$ $4x < -3$

   $x > \dfrac{-17}{6}$ and $x < \dfrac{-3}{4}$

               $\dfrac{-17}{6} < x < \dfrac{-3}{4}$

4. $4 - 2x < -6$ or $4 - 2x > 6$

   $-2x < -10$ $-2x > 2$

   $x > 5$ or $x < -1$

5. $-(x + 9) < x - 1$ and $x - 1 < x + 9$

   $-8 < 2x$ $-1 < 9$

   $x > -4$ $x > -4$

6. $2 - 4x < 0$ or $2 - 4x > 0$

   $-4x < -2$ $-4x > -2$

   $x > \dfrac{1}{2}$ or $x < \dfrac{1}{2}$

                    $x \ne \dfrac{1}{2}$

7. $-(4 + x) \le 11x$ and $11x \le 4 + x$

   $-4 \le 12x$ $10x \le 4$

   $\dfrac{-1}{3} \le x$ $x \le \dfrac{4}{10}$

   $x \ge \dfrac{-1}{3}$ $\dfrac{-1}{3} \le x \le \dfrac{2}{5}$

8. $6 - 2x < -(12 + x)$ or $6 - 2x > 12 + x$

   $-x < -18$ $3x > 6$

   $x > 18$ or $x < -2$

Page 7

1.

p	q	$p \to q$
T	T	T
T	F	F
F	T	T
F	F	T

2.

p	q	r	not q	$p \to$ not q	$(p \to$ not $q)$ and r
T	T	T	F	F	F
T	T	F	F	F	F
T	F	T	T	T	T
T	F	F	T	T	F
F	T	T	F	T	T
F	T	F	F	T	F
F	F	T	T	T	T
F	F	F	T	T	F

3.

not p	not q	r	not p or not q	r	$(\sim p$ or $\sim q) \to r$
F	F	T	F	T	T
F	F	F	F	F	T
F	T	T	T	T	T
F	T	F	T	F	F
T	F	T	T	T	T
T	F	F	T	F	F
T	T	T	T	T	T
T	T	F	T	F	F

Page 9.

1a. Suppose $n^2 + 1$ is even so $n^2 + 1 = 2k$, k is an integer. It is given that n is even so $n = 2m$, m is an integer.

Then, $(2m)^2 + 1 = 2k$

     $4m^2 + 1 = 2k$

     $2(2m + 1) = 2k$

     $2w + 1 = 2k$

where $w = 2m^2$, thus w is an integer which implies that an odd number is equal to an even number (which is a contradiction). $n^2 + 1$ is not even and it is odd.

1b. Let $n^2 - n = 12$

     $n^2 - n - 12 = 0$

     $(n - 4)(n + 3) = 0$

     $n = 4$ or -3

Because $n = 4$ by counter example 12, statement is false.

2. You did not have a precalculus test the next day. Contrapositive: If you went to bed early, then you did not have a precalculus test the next day.

3a. There exists at least one entrant that is a child and not accompanied by an adult.

3b. For all real numbers y, $y \ge 6$ or $y \le 7$.

Page 10.

1.

$$y = -2x + 7$$

$$x = -2y + 7$$

$$x - 7 = -2y$$

$$y = \frac{x}{-2} + \frac{7}{2}$$

$$f^{-1}(x) = \frac{-x}{2} + \frac{7}{2}$$

$$f(f^{-1}(x)) = -2\left(\frac{-x}{+2} + \frac{7}{2}\right) + 7 = +x - 7 + 7 = x$$

OR

$$f^{-1}(f(x)) = f^{-1}(-2x + 7)$$

$$= -\frac{(-2x + 7)}{2} + \frac{7}{2} = x$$

2.
$$y = \frac{1}{x} + 4$$
$$x = \frac{1}{y} + 4$$
$$\frac{x-4}{1} = \frac{1}{y}$$
$$y = \frac{1}{x-4}$$
$$f^{-1}(x) = \frac{1}{x-4}$$
$$f(f^{-1}(x)) = \frac{1}{\frac{1}{x-4}} + 4 = \frac{1}{1}\left(\frac{x-4}{1}\right) + 4 = x - 4 + 4 = x$$
OR
$$f^{-1}(f(x)) = f^{-1}\left(\frac{1+4}{x}\right) = \frac{1}{\frac{1}{x}+4} - 4 = x$$

3.
$$y = \frac{-1}{x+1}$$
$$\frac{x}{1} = \frac{-1}{y+1}$$
$$\frac{y+1}{1} = \frac{-1}{x}$$
$$y = \frac{-1}{x} - 1$$
$$f^{-1}(x) = -\frac{1}{x} - 1$$
$$f(f^{-1}(x)) = \frac{-1}{\left(\frac{-1}{x}-1\right)+1} = \frac{-1}{\frac{-1}{x}} = \frac{-1}{1} \cdot \frac{-x}{1} = x$$
OR
$$f^{-1}(f(x)) = f^{-1}\left(-\frac{1}{x+1}\right)$$
$$= \frac{-1}{-\frac{1}{x+1}} - 1 = x + 1 - 1 = x$$

4.
$$y = \frac{2x}{x-2}$$
$$x = \frac{2y}{y-2}$$
$$x(y-2) = 2y$$
$$xy - 2x = 2y$$
$$2y + xy = 2x$$
$$y(x-2) = 2x$$
$$y = \frac{2x}{x-2}$$
$$f^{-1}(x) = \frac{2x}{x-2}$$
$$f(f^{-1}(x)) = \frac{2\left(\frac{2x}{x-2}\right)}{\frac{2x}{x-2}-2} = \frac{\frac{4x}{x-2}}{\frac{2x \cdot 2x + 4}{x-2}} = \frac{4x}{x-2} \cdot \frac{x-2}{4} = x$$
OR
$$f^{-1}(f(x)) = f^{-1}\left(\frac{2x}{x-2}\right) = \frac{2\left(\frac{2x}{x-2}\right)}{\frac{2x}{x-2}-2} = \frac{\frac{4x}{x-2}}{\frac{4}{x-2}} = x$$

Page 12.
1. $(\ )^6$ 1 6 15 20 15 6 1
2. $(x-y)^4 = x^4 - 4x^3 y + 6x^2 y^2 - 4xy^3 + y^4$
3. $(a-3b)^3 = a^3 + 3a^2(-3b) + 3a(-3b)^2(-3b)^3$
$$= a^3 - 9a^2 b + 27ab^2 - 27b^3$$

4a. $5^6 = 15,625$
4b. $2^6 = 64$
4c. $20(5x)^3(2y)^3 \quad \therefore 20 \cdot 5^3 \cdot 2^3 = 20,000$
5. $P(x) = 7(x+y)^5$

Page 13.
1.
$$y - 5 = 3x^2 - 9x$$
$$y - 5 + \frac{27}{4} = 3\left(x^2 - 3x + \frac{9}{4}\right)$$
$$y - 5 + \frac{27}{4} = 3\left(x - \frac{3}{2}\right)^2$$
$$y + \frac{7}{4} = 3\left(x - \frac{3}{2}\right)^2$$

2.
$$y + 3 = -5x^2 + 20x$$
$$y + 3 = -5(x^2 - 4x)$$
$$-20 + y + 3 = -5(x^2 - 4x + 4)$$
$$y - 17 = -5(x - 2)^2$$

3.
$$y - 3 = x^2 + 2x$$
$$1 + y - 3 = x^2 + 2x + 1$$
$$y - 2 = (x + 1)^2$$

Page 14.
1. $(x^2 - 6x + 9) - 4(y^2 + 2y + 1) = -9 + 9 - 4$
$$\frac{(x-3)^2}{-4} - \frac{4(y+1)^2}{-4} = \frac{-4}{-4}$$
$$\frac{(y+1)^2}{1} - \frac{(x-3)^2}{4} = 1$$

2. $x^2 + 8x + 16 + y^2 - 6y + 9 = -21 + 16 + 9$
$$(x+4)^2 + (y-3)^2 = 4$$

3.
$$4x^2 - 24x + 3y^2 + 30y = -99$$
$$4(x^2 - 6x + 9) + 3(y^2 + 10y + 25) = -99 + 36 + 75$$
$$\frac{4(x-3)^2}{12} + \frac{3(y+5)^2}{12} = \frac{12}{12}$$
$$\frac{(x-3)^2}{3} + \frac{(y+5)^2}{4} = 1$$

4. $-(x^2 - 2x + 1) + 4y^2 = -2 - 1$

$$\frac{-(x-1)^2}{-3} + \frac{+4y^2}{-3} = \frac{-3}{-3}$$

$$\frac{(x-1)^2}{3} + \frac{-y^2}{\frac{3}{4}} = 1$$

Page 15.

1. $3x = -2x + 5$

$5x = 5$

$x = 1 \qquad y = 3 \qquad (1,3)$

2. $-7x = 2x^2 + 3$

$0 = 2x^2 + 7x + 3$

$0 = (2x + 1)(x + 3)$

$x = -\frac{1}{2} \qquad y = \frac{7}{2} \qquad \left(-\frac{1}{2}, \frac{7}{2}\right)$

$x = -3 \qquad y = 21 \qquad (-3, 21)$

3. $(x - 2)^2 + x^2 = 9$

$x^2 - 4x + 4 + x^2 = 9$

$2x^2 - 4x - 5 = 0$

$x = \dfrac{4 \pm \sqrt{16 + 40}}{4} \qquad \left(\dfrac{2 + \sqrt{14}}{2}, \dfrac{-2 + \sqrt{14}}{2}\right)$

$x = \dfrac{2 \pm \sqrt{14}}{2} \qquad \left(\dfrac{2 - \sqrt{14}}{2}, \dfrac{-2 - \sqrt{14}}{2}\right)$

$y = \left(\dfrac{2 \pm \sqrt{14}}{2}\right) - 2 = \left(\dfrac{-2 \pm \sqrt{14}}{2}\right)$

4. $x^2 = 3x^2 - 2$

$0 = 2x^2 - 2 = 2(x^2 - 1) = 2(x + 1)(x - 1)$

$x = 1 \qquad x = -1 \qquad\qquad (1,1)$

$y = 1 \qquad y = 1 \qquad\qquad (-1,1)$

Page 16.

1. $x^2 = 9 - y^2$

$$\frac{(9 - y^2)}{16} + \frac{y^2}{9} = 1$$

$$\frac{9}{16} - \frac{y^2}{16} + \frac{y^2}{9} = 1$$

$$144\left(\frac{-y^2}{16} + \frac{y^2}{9}\right) = \frac{7}{16}$$

$-9y^2 + 16y^2 = 63$

$7y^2 = 63$

$y^2 = 9$

$y = \pm 3 \qquad x = 0$

$(0,3) \quad (0,-3)$

2. $\qquad\qquad x^2 = 16 - y^2$

$16 - y^2 + y^2 + 4x = 11$

$4x = -5$

$x = \dfrac{-5}{4}$

$\left(\dfrac{-5}{4}\right)^2 + y^2 = 16$

$\dfrac{25}{16} + y^2 = 16$

$y^2 = \dfrac{256}{16} - \dfrac{25}{16} \qquad \left(\dfrac{-5}{4}, \dfrac{+\sqrt{231}}{4}\right)$

$y^2 = \dfrac{231}{16} \qquad\qquad \left(\dfrac{-5}{4}, \dfrac{-\sqrt{231}}{4}\right)$

$y = \dfrac{\pm\sqrt{231}}{4}$

Page 17.

1.   **2.**

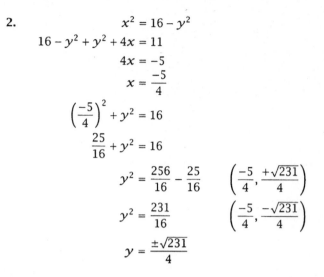

3.   **4.**

 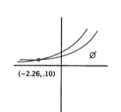

Page 20.

1. $\dfrac{a^2 b^2 c}{a^2 b^2 c^2} = \dfrac{1}{c}$

2. $\dfrac{b^2 c^6}{abc^4} = \dfrac{bc^2}{a}$

3. $\dfrac{b^8}{b^8} = 1$

4. $\dfrac{X^2 Y^3 Z^4}{X^4 Y^3 Z^2} = \dfrac{Z^2}{X^2}$

5. $\dfrac{Y^3 Z^3}{Z^3 Y^3} = 1$

6. $\dfrac{X^7 Z^6}{X^3 Y^6} = \dfrac{X^4 Z^6}{Y^6}$

Page 21.

1. $2x + 1 = x - 3$
   $x = -4$

2. $2 - 2x = x + 2$
   $0 = 3x$
   $x = 0$

3. $2 = x - 4$
   $x = 6$

4. $(3^2)^{x+7} = 3^{3-x}$
   $3^{2x+14} = 3^{3-x}$
   $2x + 14 = 3 - x$
   $3x = -11$
   $x = \dfrac{-11}{3}$

5. $(2^4)^{2x-3} = (2^3)^x$
   $4(2x - 3) = 3x$
   $8x - 12 = 3x$
   $5x = 12$
   $x = \dfrac{12}{5}$

6. $3^4 = 3^{2x-4}$
   $9 = 2x - 4$
   $2x = 8$
   $x = 4$

Page 22.

1. $\log_b 3 + 2\log_b x + \log_b 4$

2. $\log_b a + (1) + 4\log_b x + \log_b z - 2\log_b y$

3. $\log_b 2 + 2\log_b x + \log_b y + 3\log_b z - \log_b(3x - y)$

1. $\log_b \left(\dfrac{x^3 z^5}{(x-7)^2} \right)$

2. $\log_b \left(\dfrac{x^6}{(x^2+4)^5 b} \right)$

3. $2\log_b 12 - 4\log_b b + (\log_b 1) = \log_b \left(\dfrac{12^2}{b^4} \right)$

Page 23.

1. $5^2 = x \qquad x = 25$

2. $3^7 = 2x \qquad x = \dfrac{2187}{2}$

3. $4^2 = x - 1 \qquad x = 17$

4. $16 = 2^x$
   $2^4 = 2^x \qquad x = 4$

5. $400 = 20^x$
   $20^2 = 20^x \qquad x = 2$

6. $625 = 25^x$
   $5^4 = 5^{2x} \qquad x = 2$

7. $2^x = 12$
   $x \ln 2 = \ln 12$
   $x = \dfrac{\ln 12}{\ln 2} \qquad x = 3.58$

8. $32 = 2^{3x}$
   $2^5 = 2^{3x}$
   $x = \dfrac{5}{3}$

9. $x^4 = 16$
   $x^4 = 2^4 \qquad x = 2$

10. $x = \dfrac{\ln e}{\ln 2}$
    $= \dfrac{1}{\ln 2} = 1.44$

11. $(2x)^4 = 64$
    $2^4 x^4 = 64$
    $16x^4 = 64$
    $x^4 = \dfrac{64}{16} = 4$
    $x^2 = 2 \qquad b > 0$
    $x = \sqrt{2}$

Page 24.

1. $\log 5^{x+2} = \log 10^{2x}$
   $(x + 2)\log 5 = 2x$
   $x \log 5 + 2\log 5 = 2x$
   $x \log 5 - 2x = -2\log 5$
   $x = \dfrac{-2\log 5}{\log 5 - 2} = 1.074$

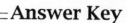

2.
$$\log 7x = \log 10^{2x-5}$$
$$x \log 7 = 2x - 5$$
$$x \log 7 - 2x = -5$$
$$x(\log 7 - 2) = -5$$
$$x = \frac{-5}{(\log 7 - 2)} = 4.330$$

Page 25.

3.
$$\log 10^x = \log 6^{x-2}$$
$$x \log 10 = (x - 2) \log 6$$
$$x = x \log 6 - 2 \log 6$$
$$x - x \log 6 = -2 \log 6$$
$$x(1 - \log 6) = -2 \log 6$$
$$x = \frac{-2 \log 6}{1 - \log 6} \qquad x = -7.015$$

4.
$$\log 7^{2x} = \log 3^{5x-2}$$
$$2x \log 7 = (5x - 2) \log 3$$
$$2x \log 7 = 5x \log 3 - 2 \log 3$$
$$2x \log 7 - 5x \log 3 = -2 \log 3$$
$$x(2 \log 7 - 5 \log 3) = -2 \log 3$$
$$x = \frac{-2 \log 3}{(2 \log 7 - 5 \log 3)} \qquad x = 1.372$$

5.
$$3x \log 5 = (2x - 3) \log 8$$
$$3x \log 5 = 2x \log 8 - 3 \log 8$$
$$3x \log 5 - 2x \log 8 = -3 \log 8$$
$$x(3 \log 5 - 2 \log 8) = -3 \log 8$$
$$x = \frac{-3 \log 8}{(3 \log 5 - 2 \log 8)} = -9.319$$

6.
$$2x \log 9 = (-x + 7) \log 3$$
$$2x \log 9 = -x \log 3 + 7 \log 3$$
$$2x \log 9 + x \log 3 = 7 \log 3$$
$$x(2 \log 9 + \log 3) = 7 \log 3$$
$$x = \frac{7 \log 3}{(2 \log 9 + \log 3)} = 1.400$$

7.
$$x \log 12 = (2x - 2) \log 6$$
$$x \log 12 = 2x \log 6 - 2 \log 6$$
$$x \log 12 - 2x \log 6 = -2 \log 6$$
$$x(\log 12 - 2 \log 6) = -2 \log 6$$
$$x = \frac{-2 \log 6}{(\log 12 - 2 \log 6)} = 3.262$$

8.
$$2x \log 11 = (x - 1) \log 102$$
$$2x \log 11 = x \log 102 - \log 102$$
$$2x \log 11 - x \log 102 = -\log 102$$
$$x(2 \log 11 - \log 102) = -\log 102$$
$$x = \frac{-\log 102}{(2 \log 11 - \log 102)} = -27.075$$

9.
$$x(\ln e) = (2x - 3) \ln 7$$
$$x = 2x \ln 7 - 3 \ln 7$$
$$x - 2x \ln 7 = -3 \ln 7$$
$$x(1 - 2 \ln 7) = -3 \ln 7$$
$$x = \frac{-3 \ln 7}{(1 - 2 \ln 7)} = 2.019$$

10.
$$2x \ln 13 = (3x + 1)(\ln e)$$
$$2x \ln 13 - 3x = 1$$
$$x(2 \ln 13 - 3) = 1$$
$$x = \frac{1}{(2 \ln 13 - 3)} = .470$$

Page 27.

1.
$$2000 = 800 \left(1 + \frac{.035}{12}\right)^{12t}$$
$$\frac{20}{8} = \left(\frac{12.035}{12}\right)^{12t}$$
$$\log \left(\frac{20}{8}\right) = 12t \log \left(\frac{12.035}{12}\right)$$
$$t = \frac{\log 2.5}{12 \log \left(\frac{12.035}{12}\right)} = 26.2 \text{ years}$$

2.
$$2500 = P \left(1 + \frac{.045}{6}\right)^{24} = P(1.0075)^{24}$$
$$P = \frac{2500}{1.0075^{24}} = \$2089.58$$

3.
$$A = 2000 \left(1 + \frac{.04}{6}\right)^{60} = \$2979.69$$

Notice difference in money in the following formula.
$$A = 2000(1.0067)^{60} = \$2985.62$$

4.
$$\frac{4000}{2000} = \frac{2000}{2000} \left(1 + \frac{.04}{6}\right)^{6t}$$
$$2 = \left(\frac{6.04}{6}\right)$$
$$\log 2 = 6t \log \left(\frac{6.04}{6}\right)$$
$$t = \frac{\log 2}{6 \log \left(\frac{6.04}{6}\right)} = 17.4 \text{ years}$$

Page 29.

1. $1200 = 300e^{r(4)}$

$\quad\quad 4 = e^{4r}$

$\quad \ln 4 = 4r \ln e$

$\quad\quad r = \dfrac{\ln 4}{4} = .3465$ or 34.66%

2. $A = 2700e^{.035(3)} = 2700e^{.105} = \$2998.92$

3. $800 = Pe^{.06(10)} = Pe^{.6} = \dfrac{800}{e^{.6}} = \$439.05$

4. $\quad\quad 1800 = 1350e^{.062t}$

$\quad\quad \dfrac{1800}{1350} = e^{.062t}$

$\quad \ln\left(\dfrac{1800}{1350}\right) = .062t\,(\ln e)$

$\quad\quad t = \dfrac{\ln\left(\frac{1800}{1350}\right)}{.062} = 4.64$ years

Page 31.

1. $\quad 250 = 500e^{k2700}$

$\quad\quad .5 = e^{k2700}$

$\quad \ln .5 = 2700k(\ln e)$

$\quad\quad k = \dfrac{\ln .5}{2700} = -.0003$

2. $\quad 2000 = 10e^{k(3.5)}$

$\quad\quad 200 = e^{k(3.5)}$

$\quad \ln 200 = 3.5k(\ln e)$

$\quad\quad k = \dfrac{\ln 200}{3.5} = 1.5138$

3. $\quad 10 = 50e^{-.345t}$

$\quad\quad \dfrac{1}{5} = e^{-.345t}$

$\quad \ln \dfrac{1}{5} = -.345t(\ln e)$

$\quad\quad t = \dfrac{\ln 2}{-.345} = 4.7$ years

4. $A = 100e^{(2.5)10} = 100e^{25} = 100(7.2 \times 10^{10}) = 7.2 \times 10^{12}$

Page 33.

1. $4^2 + 5^2 + 6^2 + 7^2 + 8^2 = 190$
2. $3^2 + 3^3 + 3^4 + 3^5 + 3^6 = 9 + 27 + 81 + 243 + 729 = 1089$
3. $8 + 7 + 6 + 5 + 4 + 3 = 33$
1. $tn = 3 + (n-1)5$

$\quad\quad tn = 5n - 2 \quad\quad \displaystyle\sum_{n=1}^{4} 5n - 2$

2. $tn = -5 + (n-1)4$

$\quad tn = -5 + 4n - 4$

$\quad tn = 4n - 9 \quad\quad \displaystyle\sum_{n=1}^{4} 4n - 9$

Page 34.

1. $a = 3 \quad n = 8 \quad r = 2$

$\quad s_8 = \dfrac{3(1 - 2^8)}{1 - 2} = \dfrac{3(-255)}{-1} = 765$

2. $s_5 = \dfrac{1}{2}\left(\dfrac{1 - \left(\frac{1}{2}\right)^5}{1 - \frac{1}{2}}\right) = \dfrac{1}{2}\dfrac{\left(1 - \left(\frac{1}{2}\right)^5\right)}{\frac{1}{2}}$

$\quad = 1 - \left(\dfrac{1}{2}\right)^5 = 1 - \dfrac{1}{32} = \dfrac{31}{32}$

Page 35.

1. $S = \dfrac{9}{1 - r} = |r| < 1 \quad r = 2$

The sum does not exist (infinite) because $|r| > 1$.

2. $S = \dfrac{9}{1 - r} \quad\quad r = \dfrac{1}{3}$

$\quad S = \dfrac{\frac{3}{2}}{1 - \frac{1}{3}} = \dfrac{\frac{3}{2}}{\frac{2}{3}} = \dfrac{3}{2} \cdot \dfrac{3}{2} = \dfrac{9}{4}$

3. $S = \dfrac{9}{1 - r} \quad\quad r = \dfrac{-1}{3}$

$\quad S = \dfrac{-2}{1 - \left(-\frac{1}{3}\right)} = \dfrac{-2}{\frac{4}{3}} = \dfrac{-2}{1} \cdot \dfrac{3}{4} = \dfrac{-6}{4} = -1.5$ or $\dfrac{-3}{2}$

Page 37.

1. $\displaystyle\sum_{n=1}^{6} 4n - 3 \quad tn = 1 + (n-1)9 = 4n - 3$

2. $\displaystyle\sum_{n=1}^{6} -3(-2)^{n-1} \quad\quad tn = ar^{n-1}$

$\quad\quad\quad\quad\quad\quad\quad\quad tn = -3(-2)^{n-1}$

3. $0 + 0 + 2 + 6 + 8$
4. $8 - 15 + 24 - 35 + 48 - 63 + 80 = 47$
5a. $7, 5, 3, 1, -1$
5b. $tn = a_1 + (n-1)d$

$\quad\quad tn = 7 + (n-1)2 = 2n + 5$

Page 39.

1. Let $s = \{n \in N: a_n = 2^n + 1\}$

1. Show $1 \in S$ $a_1 = 2^1 + 1 = 3$ true $1 \in S$
2. Assume $x \in S$ $9x = 2^x + 1$
   Prove $x + 1 \in S$ $a_{x+1} = 2^{x+1} + 1$
3. Proof: $a_{x+1} = 2a_x - 1$
       $a_x = 2^x + 1$
       $a_{x+1} = 2(2^x + 1) - 1$ (substitute)
       $a_{x+1} = 2 \cdot 2^x + 2 - 1$
       $a_{x+1} = 2^{x+1} + 1$ $\therefore S = N$

2. Let $S = \left\{ n \in N: a_n = 5\left(\frac{1}{2}\right)^{n-1} \right\}$

1. Show $1 \in S$ $a_1 = 5\left(\frac{1}{2}\right)^{1-1} = 5 \cdot 1 = 5$ true
2. Assume $x \in S$ $a_x = 5\left(\frac{1}{2}\right)^{x-1}$
   Prove $x + 1 \in S$ $a_{x+1} = 5\left(\frac{1}{2}\right)^{(x+1)-1}$

2. continued

3. Proof: $a_{x+1} = \dfrac{a_x}{2}$

       $a_x = 5\left(\frac{1}{2}\right)^{x-1}$

       $a_{x+1} = \dfrac{5\left(\frac{1}{2}\right)^{(x-1)}}{2}$

       $= 5\left(\frac{1}{2}\right)^{(x-1)}\left(\frac{1}{2}\right)^1$ (substitute)

       $= 5\left(\frac{1}{2}\right)^{(x+1)-1}$ $\therefore S = N$

3. Let $S = \left\{ n \in N: a_n = \dfrac{n}{2} - \dfrac{a}{2} \right\}$

1. Show $1 \in S$ $a_1 = \dfrac{1}{2} - \dfrac{9}{8} = \dfrac{-8}{2} = -4$ true $1 \in S$
2. Assume $x \in S$ $a_x = \dfrac{x}{2} - \dfrac{9}{2}$
   Prove $x + 1 \in S$ $a_{x+1} = \dfrac{x+1}{2} - \dfrac{9}{2}$
3. Proof: $a_{x+1} = a_x + \dfrac{1}{2}$

       $a_x = \dfrac{x}{2} - \dfrac{9}{2}$

       $a_{x+1} = \dfrac{x}{2} - \dfrac{9}{2} + \dfrac{1}{2}$ (substitute)

       $a_{x+1} = \left(\dfrac{x}{2} + \dfrac{1}{2}\right) - \dfrac{9}{2} = \left(\dfrac{x+1}{2}\right) - \dfrac{9}{2}$ $\therefore S = N$

Page 40.

1. Let $S = \left\{ n \in N: \dfrac{1}{2} + \dfrac{1}{6} + \dfrac{1}{12} + \cdots + \dfrac{1}{n(n+1)} = \dfrac{n}{n+1} \right\}$

1. Show $1 \in S$ $\dfrac{1}{2} = \dfrac{1}{1(1+1)} = \dfrac{1}{2}$ true $1 \in S$
2. Assume $x \in S$ $\dfrac{1}{2} + \dfrac{1}{6} + \dfrac{1}{12} + \cdots + \dfrac{1}{x(x+1)} = \dfrac{x}{x+1}$
   Prove $x + 1 \in S$ $\dfrac{1}{2} + \dfrac{1}{6} + \dfrac{1}{12} + \cdots + \dfrac{1}{x(x+1)} + \dfrac{1}{(x+1)[(x+1)+1]} = \dfrac{x+1}{(x+1)+1} = \dfrac{x+1}{x+2}$
3. Proof: $\dfrac{1}{2} + \dfrac{1}{6} + \dfrac{1}{12} + \cdots + \dfrac{1}{x(x+1)} + = \dfrac{1}{(x+[(x+1)+1]} = \dfrac{x}{x+1} + \dfrac{1}{(x+1)[(x+1)+1]}$

       $= \dfrac{x}{(x+1)} + \dfrac{(x+2)}{(x+2)} + \dfrac{1}{(x+1)(x+2)} = \dfrac{x^2 + 2x + 1}{(x+1)(x+2)}$

       $= \dfrac{(x+1)(x+1)}{(x+1)(x+2)} = \dfrac{(x+1)}{(x+2)}$

       $\therefore S = N$

2. Let $S = \left\{ n \in N : 1^3 + 2^3 + 3^3 + \ldots n^3 = \dfrac{[n(n+1)]^2}{4} \right\}$

1. Show $1 \in S$ $\quad \dfrac{[1(1+1)]^2}{4} = \dfrac{2^2}{4} = \dfrac{4}{4} = 1 = 1^3$ yes $1 \in S$

2. Assume $x \in S$ $\quad 1^3 + 2^3 + 3^3 + \ldots x^3 = \dfrac{[x(x+1)]^2}{4}$

   Prove $x + 1 \in S$ $\quad 1^3 + 2^3 + 3^3 + \ldots x^3 + (x+1)^3 = \dfrac{[(x+1)(x+2)]^2}{4} = \dfrac{(x^2 + 3x + 2)^2}{4}$

3. Proof: $\quad 1^3 + 2^3 + 3^3 + \ldots + x^3 + (x+1)^3 = \dfrac{[x(x+1)]^2}{4} + (x+1)^3 = \dfrac{(x^2 + x)^2}{4} + x^3 + 3x^2 + 3x + 1$

$$= \dfrac{x^4 + 2x^3 + x^2 + 4x^3 + 12x^2 + 12x + 4}{4}$$

$$= \dfrac{x^4 + 6x^3 + 13x^2 + 12x + x^4}{4} = \dfrac{(x^2 + 3x + 2)^2}{4} \qquad \therefore S = N$$

Page 43.

1. $(-2)^3 - 3(-2) + 12 = 10$

2. no limit

3. $3(x + 3) = 18$

4. $\dfrac{(x + 3)(x + 4)}{(x + 3)} = 1$

5. $\dfrac{(x + 1)(x - 6)}{(x - 6)} = 7$

6. $\dfrac{(x - 1)(x^2 + x + 1)}{(x + 1)(x - 1)} = \dfrac{3}{2}$

Page 44.

1. 3 $\qquad$ **2.** 0 $\qquad$ **3.** -4

4. does not exist $\qquad$ **5.** -1 $\qquad$ **6.** -1

Page 45.

1. $\dfrac{(x - 1)}{(x - 6)} = \dfrac{-2}{-7}$

$\qquad x \neq -1 \quad \left(-1, \frac{2}{7}\right)$

2. $\dfrac{(x + 1)}{(x + 5)} = \dfrac{6}{10}$

$\qquad x \neq 5 \quad \left(5, \frac{3}{5}\right)$

3. $\dfrac{(x + 1)}{(x - 9)} = \dfrac{-8}{-18}$

$\qquad x \neq -9 \quad \left(-9, \frac{4}{9}\right)$

Page 46.

1. $\dfrac{(x + 3)(x - 3)}{(x + 1)(x - 3)} \qquad x = -1$

2. $\dfrac{(x - 4)(x + 1)}{(x - 4)(x + 4)} \qquad x = -4$

3. $\dfrac{(x + 6)(x + 1)}{(x + 1)(x - 1)} \qquad x = 1$

4. $\dfrac{(x - 2)(x - 2)}{(x - 2)(x + 1)} \qquad x = -1$

5. $\dfrac{x}{(x - 1)(x + 1)} \qquad x = 1$ or $x = -1$

6. $\dfrac{(x - 2)(x + 2)}{(x - 3)(x + 3)} \qquad x = 3$ or $x = -3$

7. $x = -1$

8. $x = \dfrac{-1}{2}$

Page 48.

1. $\displaystyle\lim_{x \to \infty} f(x) = \dfrac{1}{3}$ horizontal asymptote

$\qquad y = \dfrac{1}{3}$

2.
$$\begin{array}{r} x - 3 \\ x - 3 \overline{\smash{\big)}\, x^2 - 6x + 5} \\ \underline{-x^2 + 3x} \\ -3x + 5 \end{array}$$

$\qquad y = x - 3$ oblique asymptote

3. $\displaystyle\lim_{x \to \infty} f(x) = 0$ horizontal asymptote

$\qquad y = 0$

4. $\displaystyle\lim_{x \to \infty} f(x) =$ does not exist

5. $\displaystyle\lim_{x \to \infty} f(x) = 0$ horizontal asymptote

$\qquad y = 0$

6. $\lim\limits_{x \to \infty} f(x) = \dfrac{9}{3} = 3$ horizontal asymptote

$y = 3$

7. $\lim\limits_{x \to \infty} f(x) = \dfrac{5}{2}$ horizontal asymptote

$y = \dfrac{5}{2}$

8.

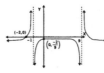

$y = x$ is an oblique asymptote

Page 50.

1. $y = 0$ horizontal asymptote

$\left(0, \dfrac{2}{9}\right) \ (-2, 0)$

$\dfrac{x + 2}{(x - 9)(x + 1)}$ $\quad x = 9, -1$ vertical asymptotes

2. $\dfrac{(x - 2)(x + 2)}{(x - 2)(x - 2)}$ $\quad y = 1$ horizontal asymptote

$(0, -1) \quad (x^2 - 4) = 0 \quad x = +2$
$(-2, 0) \quad x = -2, 2 \quad$ vertical asymptote

Note: In original equation $f(x) = \dfrac{0}{0}$, but there is no

point of discontinuity because in reduced equation

$g(x) = \dfrac{x + 2}{x - 2}$ and $g(2)$ is undefined.

3. $\dfrac{x^2}{(x - 2)(x - 4)}$ $\quad y = 1$ horizontal
$x = 0$
$y = 0 \quad x = 2, 4$
vertical

$f(3) = \dfrac{9}{9 - 18 + 8} = \dfrac{9}{1} = -9$

4. $\dfrac{(x - 4)(x - 1)}{(x - 4)}$

$x = 0 \qquad y = 0$
$y = -1 \qquad x = 1$

Page 51.

1. sum $14 - 6i$
difference $8 + 2i$
product $25 - 50i$

2. sum $8 + 6i$
difference $6 + 8i$
product 14

3. sum $11 + 7i$
difference $1 - 3i$
product $20 + 40i$

4. sum $8 - 6i$
difference $8 - 12i$
product $27 + 24i$

5. sum $39 + 9i$
difference $15 - 35i$
product $610 + 438i$

6. sum 20
difference $2\sqrt{2}i$
product 102

Page 52.

1. $\dfrac{(6 + 6i)}{(6 + 6i)} = \dfrac{18 + 18 - 18i + 18i}{72}$

$\dfrac{36}{72} = \dfrac{1}{2}$

2. $\dfrac{(1 - i)}{(1 - i)} = \dfrac{2 + 7 + 7i - 2i}{2}$

$= \dfrac{9}{2} + \dfrac{5i}{2}$

3. $\dfrac{(-2i)}{(-2i)} = \dfrac{-2 - 24i}{4}$

$= \dfrac{-1}{2} - 6i$

4. $\dfrac{(3 - 4i)}{(3 - 4i)} = \dfrac{15 + 20 + 15i - 20i}{25}$

$\dfrac{35}{25} - \dfrac{5}{25}i = \dfrac{7}{5} - \dfrac{1}{5}i$

5. $\dfrac{(7 - 7i)}{(7 - 7i)} = \dfrac{154 - 77 - 77i - 15i}{98}$

$\dfrac{77 - 231i}{98} = \dfrac{77}{98} - \dfrac{231i}{98}$

$= \dfrac{11}{14} - \dfrac{33}{14}i$

6. $\dfrac{(16 + 8i)}{(16 + 8i)} = \dfrac{400 - 64 + 128i + 200i}{320}$

$\dfrac{336}{320} + \dfrac{328}{320}i = \dfrac{21}{20} + \dfrac{41}{40}i$

Page 53.

1. $|z| = \sqrt{58}$

$\tan^{-1}\left(\dfrac{-7}{3}\right) = -66.8°$

$\left(\sqrt{58}, -66.8°\right)$

2. $|z| = \sqrt{85}$

$\tan^{-1}\left(\dfrac{6}{7}\right) = 40.6°$

$\left(\sqrt{85}, 40.6°\right)$

3. $|z| = 5\sqrt{2}$
$\theta = -45°$
$\left(5\sqrt{2}, -45°\right)$

4. $\sqrt{45} = 3\sqrt{5}$
$\tan^{-1}\left(\dfrac{3}{-6}\right) + 180° = -26.57° + 180°$ second quadrant
$\left(3\sqrt{5}, 153.4°\right)$

5. $|z| = \sqrt{11}$
$\theta = \tan^{-1}\left(\dfrac{-\sqrt{2}}{3}\right) = -25.24°$
$\left(\sqrt{11}, -25.2°\right)$

6. $|z| = z$
$\theta = 45°$
$(2, 45°)$

7. $|z| = 2$
$\tan\left(\dfrac{-1}{\sqrt{3}}\right) = -30$
$(2, -30°)$

8. $|z| = 5$
$\tan\left(\dfrac{-3}{4}\right) = -36.87$
$(5, 143.1°)$

Page 54.

1. $z = \sqrt{13}(\cos 30° + i\sin 30)$
$z = \sqrt{13}\left(\dfrac{\sqrt{3}}{2} + \dfrac{1}{2}i\right) = \dfrac{\sqrt{39}}{2} + \dfrac{\sqrt{13}}{2}i$

2. $z = 8(\cos 60° + i\sin 60°)$
$z = 8\left(\dfrac{1}{2} + \dfrac{\sqrt{3}}{2}i\right) = 4 + 4\sqrt{3}i$

3. $z = 10(\cos(-135°) + i\sin(-135°))$
$z = 10\left(\dfrac{-\sqrt{2}}{2} + \dfrac{\sqrt{2}}{2}i\right) = -5\sqrt{2} - 5\sqrt{2}i$

4. $z = 3(\cos 120° + i\sin 120°)$
$z = 3\left(-\dfrac{1}{2} + \dfrac{\sqrt{3}}{2}i\right) = \dfrac{-3}{2} + \dfrac{3\sqrt{3}}{2}i$

5. $z = 35(\cos 57° + i\sin 57°)$
$z = 35(.544 + i(.839))$
$z = 19.06 + 29.35i$

6. $z = 9(\cos 22.5° + i\sin 22.5°)$
$z = 9(.9238 + i(.3827))$
$z = 8.31 + 3.44i$

Page 55.

1. $35(\cos 95° + i\sin 95°)$
$\dfrac{7}{5}(\cos 25° + i\sin 25°)$

2. $5(\cos 180° + i\sin 180°)$
$20(\cos 20° + i\sin 20°)$

3. $3(\cos 120° + i\sin 120°)$
$\dfrac{1}{3}(\cos -60° + i\sin -60°)$

4. $60(\cos 120° + i\sin 120°)$
$\dfrac{5}{12}(\cos 30° + i\sin 30°)$

Page 56.

1a. $z^3 = 6^3(\cos 60° + i\sin 60°)$
$z^3 = 216(\cos 60° + i\sin 60°)$

1b. $z^6 = 6^6(\cos 120° + i\sin 120°)$
$z^6 = 46,656(\cos 120° + i\sin 120°)$

2a. $z^{\frac{1}{3}} = 64^{\frac{1}{3}}(\cos 16° + i\sin 16°) = 4(\cos 16° + i\sin 16°)$
$z^{\frac{1}{3}} = 64^{\frac{1}{3}}(\cos 136° + i\sin 136°) = 4(\cos 136° + i\sin 136°)$
$z^{\frac{1}{3}} = 64^{\frac{1}{3}}(\cos 256° + i\sin 256°) = 4(\cos 256° + i\sin 256°)$

2b. $z^{\frac{1}{8}} = 64^{\frac{1}{8}}(\cos 6° + i\sin 6°) = 1.68(\cos 6° + i\sin 6°)$
$z^{\frac{1}{8}} = 1.68(\cos 51° + i\sin 51°)$
$z^{\frac{1}{8}} = 1.68(\cos 96° + i\sin 96°)$
$z^{\frac{1}{8}} = 1.68(\cos 141° + i\sin 141°)$
$z^{\frac{1}{8}} = 1.68(\cos 186° + i\sin 186°)$
$z^{\frac{1}{8}} = 1.68(\cos 231° + i\sin 231°)$
$z^{\frac{1}{8}} = 1.68(\cos 276° + i\sin 276°)$
$z^{\frac{1}{8}} = 1.68(\cos 321° + i\sin 321°)$

2c. $z^{\frac{1}{2}} = 64^{\frac{1}{2}}(\cos 24° + i\sin 24°) = 8(\cos 24° + i\sin 24°)$
$z^{\frac{1}{2}} = 8(\cos 204° + i\sin 204°)$

Page 58.

1. $\sin A = \dfrac{3}{5}$ $\cos A = \dfrac{4}{5}$ $\tan A = \dfrac{3}{4}$

 $\cot A = \dfrac{4}{3}$ $\sec A = \dfrac{5}{4}$ $\csc A = \dfrac{5}{3}$

Page 59.

2. $\sin A = \dfrac{5}{13}$ $\cos A = \dfrac{12}{13}$ $\tan A = \dfrac{5}{12}$

 $\cot A = \dfrac{12}{5}$ $\sec A = \dfrac{13}{12}$ $\csc A = \dfrac{13}{5}$

3. $\sin B = \dfrac{15}{17}$ $\cos B = \dfrac{8}{17}$ $\tan B = \dfrac{15}{8}$

 $\cot B = \dfrac{8}{15}$ $\sec B = \dfrac{17}{8}$ $\csc B = \dfrac{17}{15}$

4. $\sin A = \dfrac{10}{22.36}$ $\sin B = \dfrac{20}{22.36}$

 $\cos A = \dfrac{20}{22.36}$ $\cos B = \dfrac{10}{22.36}$

 $\tan A = \dfrac{10}{20}$ $\tan B = \dfrac{20}{10}$

 $\cot A = \dfrac{20}{10}$ $\cot B = \dfrac{10}{20}$

 $\sec A = \dfrac{22.36}{20}$ $\sec B = \dfrac{22.36}{10}$

 $\csc A = \dfrac{22.36}{10}$ $\csc B = \dfrac{22.36}{20}$

5. $\sin A = \cos B$ $\cos A = \sin B$

 $\tan A = \cot B$ $\cot A = \tan B$

 $\sec A = \csc B$ $\csc A = \sec B$

 The two angles are complimentary so that the trig function of one is the cofunction of the other.

Page 61.

1. $\sin y = \dfrac{\sqrt{4 - x^2}}{2}$ $\cot y = \dfrac{x}{\sqrt{4 - x^2}}$

 $\cos y = \dfrac{x}{2}$ $\sec y = \dfrac{2}{x}$

 $\tan y = \dfrac{\sqrt{4 - x^2}}{x}$ $\csc y = \dfrac{2}{\sqrt{4 - x^2}}$

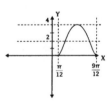

2. $\sin y = \dfrac{2}{x}$ $\cot y = \dfrac{\sqrt{x^2 - 4}}{2}$

 $\cos y = \dfrac{\sqrt{x^2 - 4}}{x}$ $\sec y = \dfrac{x}{\sqrt{x^2 - 4}}$

 $\tan y = \dfrac{2}{\sqrt{x^2 - 4}}$ $\csc y = \dfrac{x}{2}$

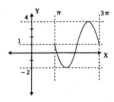

3. $\sin y = \dfrac{\sqrt{4x^2 - 9}}{2x}$ $\cot y = \dfrac{3}{\sqrt{4x^2 - 9}}$

 $\cos y = \dfrac{3}{2x}$ $\sec y = \dfrac{2x}{3}$

 $\tan y = \dfrac{\sqrt{4x^2 - 9}}{3}$ $\csc y = \dfrac{2x}{\sqrt{4x^2 - 9}}$

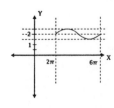

4. $\sin y = \dfrac{8}{\sqrt{x^2 + 64}}$ $\cot y = \dfrac{x}{8}$

 $\cos y = \dfrac{x}{\sqrt{x^2 + 64}}$ $\sec y = \dfrac{\sqrt{x^2 + 64}}{x}$

 $\tan y = \dfrac{8}{x}$ $\csc y = \dfrac{\sqrt{x^2 + 64}}{8}$

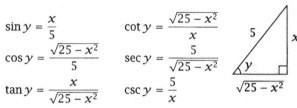

5. $\sin y = \dfrac{x}{5}$ $\cot y = \dfrac{\sqrt{25 - x^2}}{x}$

 $\cos y = \dfrac{\sqrt{25 - x^2}}{5}$ $\sec y = \dfrac{5}{\sqrt{25 - x^2}}$

 $\tan y = \dfrac{x}{\sqrt{25 - x^2}}$ $\csc y = \dfrac{5}{x}$

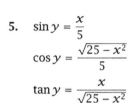

6. $\sin y = \dfrac{x}{\sqrt{x^2 + 1}}$ $\cot y = \dfrac{1}{x}$

 $\cos y = \dfrac{1}{\sqrt{x^2 + 1}}$ $\sec y = \sqrt{x^2 + 1}$

 $\tan y = \dfrac{x}{1} = x$ $\csc y = \dfrac{\sqrt{x^2 + 1}}{x}$

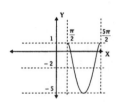

Page 62.

1. centerline $+1$

 amplitude 1

 phase shift $-\dfrac{C}{B} = \dfrac{\pi}{3}$ $\quad x = \dfrac{\pi}{3}$

 period $\dfrac{2\pi}{3}$

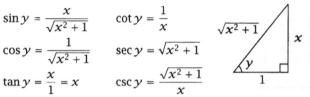

Page 63.

2. centerline -2

 amplitude 3

 phase shift $\dfrac{\pi}{2}$

 period $\dfrac{2\pi}{1}$

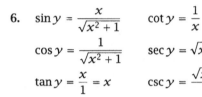

3. centerline 2

 amplitude 2

 phase shift $\dfrac{\pi}{12}$

 period $\dfrac{2\pi}{12}$

4. centerline 1

 amplitude 3

 phase shift π

 period 2π

5. centerline 2

 amplitude $\dfrac{1}{2}$

 phase shift 2π

 period $\dfrac{2\pi}{\frac{1}{2}} = 4\pi$

Page 64.

1. $\sec 3x = \dfrac{1}{\cos 3x}$

   $y = \cos 3x$

   period $\dfrac{2\pi}{3}$

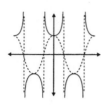

2. $y = \cot 4x = \dfrac{\cos 4x}{\sin 4x}$

   $y = \sin 4x$

   period $\dfrac{2\pi}{4} = \dfrac{\pi}{2}$

3. $y = \csc \dfrac{x}{2} = \dfrac{1}{\sin\left(\frac{x}{2}\right)}$

   $y = \sin \frac{x}{2}$

   period $\dfrac{2\pi}{\frac{1}{2}} = 4\pi$

Page 66.

1. $\dfrac{\tan^2 x}{\sec x + 1} = \dfrac{\tan^2 x}{\sec x + 1}\left(\dfrac{\sec x - 1}{\sec x - 1}\right)$

   $\qquad = \dfrac{\tan^2 x (\sec x - 1)}{\sec^2 x - 1}$

   $\qquad = \dfrac{\tan^2 x (\sec x - 1)}{\tan^2 x}$

   $\qquad = \sec x - 1$

2. $\dfrac{\frac{\sin x}{\cos x} + \frac{\cos x}{\sin x}}{1/\sin^2 x} = \dfrac{\sin x}{\cos x}$

   $\dfrac{\frac{\sin^2 x + \cos^2 x}{\cos x \sin x}}{1/\sin^2 x} = \dfrac{\sin x}{\cos x}$

   $\dfrac{\frac{1}{\cos x \sin x}}{1/\sin^2 x} = \dfrac{\sin x}{\cos x}$

   $\dfrac{1}{\cos x \sin x} \cdot \dfrac{\sin^2 x}{1} = \dfrac{\sin x}{\cos x}$

   $\dfrac{\sin x}{\cos x} = \dfrac{\sin x}{\cos x}$

Page 69.

1.
   a. $\sin x = \dfrac{-7}{\sqrt{65}}$ or $\dfrac{-7\sqrt{65}}{65}$

   b. $\cos x = \dfrac{-4}{\sqrt{65}}$ or $\dfrac{-4\sqrt{65}}{65}$

   c. $\tan x = \dfrac{7}{4}$

   d. $\sec x = \dfrac{-\sqrt{65}}{4}$

   e. $\csc x = \dfrac{-\sqrt{65}}{7}$

2. $x = \sin^{-1}, 592$

   $x = 36.3°$ 1st quadrant

   $x = 180° - 36.3° = 143.7°$ 2nd quadrant

   $2x = 2(143.7°) = 287.4°$ $\sin 2x = \sin 287.4° = -.9542$

3. $\cos x = a$

   $5a^2 + 4a - 1 = 0$

   $(5a - 1)(a + 1) = 0$

   $a = \dfrac{1}{5}, -1$

   $0 \le x \le 360°$

   $\cos x = \dfrac{1}{5}$

   $x = \cos^{-1}\left(\dfrac{1}{5}\right)$

   $\quad = -78.46°$ or $78.46° + 360°n$

   $x = 360° - 78.46°$

   $\quad = 281.54°$ or $-78.46° + 360°n$

   $\cos x = -1$

   $x = \cos^{-1}(-1) = 180°$ or $180° + 360°n$

4. $\sin x = \dfrac{4}{5}$

   $x = \sin^{-1}\left(\dfrac{9}{5}\right)$

   $x = .9273$

   $x = \pi - .9273$

   $x = 2.214$

   $(0 < x < .9273$ or $2.214 < x < 2\pi)$

Page 70.

1a. To solve a trig I.D., sometimes you convert everything to sin and cos. Generally, the next step will involve factoring the common denominator or some other algebra operation. Always look for possible Pythagorean substitutions. Transform the more complicated side to the simpler side. Never cross the equals sign.

1b. $\tan x(\tan x + \cot x) = \tan^2 x + \tan x \cot x$

   $\qquad = \tan^2 x + \dfrac{\sin x}{\cos x} \cdot \dfrac{\cos x}{\sin x}$

   $\qquad = \tan^2 x + 1$

   $\qquad = \sec^2 x$

2a. $\dfrac{\pi}{3} = \dfrac{4\pi}{12} \qquad \dfrac{\pi}{4} = \dfrac{3\pi}{12}$

   $\cos\left(\dfrac{7\pi}{12}\right) = \cos\left(\dfrac{\pi}{3} + \dfrac{\pi}{4}\right)$

   $\qquad = \cos \dfrac{\pi}{3} \cos \dfrac{\pi}{4} - \sin \dfrac{\pi}{3} \sin \dfrac{\pi}{4}$

   $\dfrac{1}{2} \cdot \dfrac{\sqrt{2}}{2} - \dfrac{\sqrt{3}}{2} \dfrac{\sqrt{2}}{2} = \dfrac{\sqrt{2} - \sqrt{6}}{4} = -.2588$

3a.
$$\cos 2x = 2\cos^2 x - 1$$
$$\cos 2x + 1 = 2\cos^2 x$$
$$\frac{\cos 2x + 1}{2} = \cos^2 x$$
$$\cos^2 x = \frac{\cos 2x + 1}{2}$$
$$\cos x = \pm\sqrt{\frac{\cos 2x + 1}{2}}$$

3b.
$$\cos 2x = 1 - 2\sin^2 x$$
$$\cos 2x - 1 = -2\sin^2 x$$
$$\frac{\cos 2x - 1}{-2} = \sin^2 x$$
$$\sin^2 x = \frac{1 - \cos 2x}{2}$$
$$\sin x = \pm\sqrt{\frac{1 - \cos 2x}{2}}$$

Page 71.

1a. domain $-\dfrac{\pi}{2} \le x \le \dfrac{\pi}{2}$

range $-1 \le y \le 1$

1b. domain $-1 \le x \le 1$

range $-\dfrac{\pi}{2} \le y \le \dfrac{\pi}{2}$

2a. domain $-\dfrac{\pi}{2} < x < \dfrac{\pi}{2}$

range $-\infty < y < \infty$

2b. domain $-\infty < x < \infty$

range $-\dfrac{\pi}{2} < y < \dfrac{\pi}{2}$

3a. domain $0 \le x \le \pi$

range $-1 \le y \le 1$

3b. domain $-1 \le x \le 1$

range $0 \le y \le \pi$

Page 74.

1.

$$3\,|\ \ 5 \quad -3 \quad +5 \quad +0 \quad -10$$
$$\underline{\ +15 \quad +36 \quad +123 \quad +369}$$
$$5 \quad +12 \quad +41 \quad +123 \quad +359 \qquad f(3) = 359$$

2.

$$-2\,|\ \ 3 \quad -6 \quad +2 \quad +9 \quad -1$$
$$\underline{\ -6 \quad +24 \quad -52 \quad +86}$$
$$3 \quad -12 \quad +26 \quad -43 \quad +87$$

No, -2 is not a root. Also, -2 does not satisfy the rational root theorem.

3.

$$2\,|\ \ -4 \quad -1 \quad +7 \quad +3 \quad -11 \qquad P(2) = -49$$
$$\underline{\ -8 \quad -18 \quad -22 \quad -38} \qquad (2, -49)$$
$$-4 \quad -9 \quad -11 \quad -19 \quad -49$$

4.

$$-2\,|\ \ 9 \quad -12 \quad +17 \quad +5 \quad -25$$
$$\underline{\ -18 \quad +60 \quad -154 \quad +298}$$
$$9 \quad -30 \quad +77 \quad -149 \quad +273$$
$9x^3 - 30x^2 + 77x - 149$ is the reduced equation.

5.

$$-3\,|\ \ 3 \quad -9 \quad -1 \quad +12 \quad +6 \quad -36 \qquad P(-3) = -1377$$
$$\underline{\ -9 \quad +54 \quad -159 \quad +441 \quad -1341}$$
$$3 \quad -18 \quad +53 \quad -147 \quad +447 \quad -1377$$

Page 75.

1.
$$n = x^2$$
$$x^2 - 5n + 4 = 0$$
$$(n - 4)(n - 1) = 0$$
$$n = 4,\ 1$$
$$x^2 = 4 \qquad x^2 = 1$$
$$x = \pm 2 \qquad x = \pm 1$$

2.
$$2n^2 - n - 10 = 0$$
$$(2n - 5)(n + 2) = 0$$
$$n = \frac{5}{2},\ -2$$
$$x^2 = \frac{5}{2} \qquad x^2 = -2$$
$$x = \pm\sqrt{\frac{5}{2}} \qquad x = \pm\sqrt{2}i$$

3.
$$3n^2 - 8n - 3 = 0$$
$$(3n + 1)(n - 3) = 0$$
$$n = \frac{-1}{3},\ 3$$
$$x^2 = \frac{-1}{3} \qquad x^2 = 3$$
$$x = \pm\sqrt{\frac{1}{3}}i \qquad x = \pm\sqrt{3}$$

4.
$$5n^2 - 2n - 3 = 0$$
$$(5n + 3)(n - 1) = 0$$
$$n = \frac{-3}{5},\ 1$$
$$x^2 = \frac{-3}{5} \qquad x^2 = 1$$
$$x = \pm\sqrt{\frac{3}{5}}i \qquad x = \pm 1$$

Page 76.

1.
$$(\sin x)^2 = n$$
$$n^2 - 5n + 4 = 0$$
$$(n-1)(n-4) = 0$$
$$n = 1, 4 \quad \text{so 4 is not in the domain of } \sin x$$

$$\sin^2 x = 1 \qquad \sin^2 x = 4$$
$$\sin x = \pm 1 \qquad \sin x = \pm 2$$
$$x = \sin^{-1} \qquad \sin x \geq 1$$
$$1 = 90° \text{ or } \sin^{-1} -1 = 270°$$

2.
$$\cos^2 x = n$$
$$2n^2 - n - 10 = 0$$
$$(2n-5)(n+2) = 0$$
$$n = \frac{5}{2} \text{ or } n = 2$$
$$\text{but } -1 \leq \cos x \leq 1$$
$$\therefore \text{ there are no solutions}$$

3.
$$(\log x)^2 = n$$
$$n^2 - 9n + 8 = 0$$
$$(n-1)(n-8) = 0$$
$$n = 1, 8$$
$$(\log x)^2 = 8$$
$$\log x = \pm\sqrt{8}$$
$$x = 10^{\sqrt{8}} \text{ or } 10^{-\sqrt{8}}$$
$$(\log x)^2 = 1$$
$$\log x = \pm 1$$
$$x = 10^1 = 10$$
$$x = 10^{-1} = \frac{1}{10}$$

4.
$$5n^2 - 23n - 10 = 0$$
$$(5n+2)(n-5) = 0$$
$$n = \frac{-2}{5}, 5$$
$$x = \pm\sqrt{\frac{2}{5}}\,i$$
$$x = \pm\sqrt{5}$$

5.
$$n = x^4 \quad \text{or} \quad n = -1$$
$$n^2 - 5n - 6 = 0 \qquad x^4 \neq 1$$
$$(n-6)(n+1) = 0 \qquad x^2 = \pm\sqrt{-1} = \pm i$$
$$x^4 = 6 \qquad x = \pm\sqrt{i} \text{ or } \pm\sqrt{-i}$$
$$x^2 = \pm\sqrt{6}$$
$$x = \pm\sqrt{\sqrt{6}}$$
$$x = \pm\sqrt{\sqrt{6}}\,i$$

6.
$$n = x^3$$
$$2n^2 - 5n - 12 = 0$$
$$(2n+3)(n-4) = 0$$
$$n = \frac{-3}{2}, 4$$
$$x^3 = \frac{-3}{2} \qquad x^3 = 4$$
$$x = \sqrt[3]{\frac{-3}{2}} \qquad x = \sqrt[3]{4}$$
Plus 4 imaginary roots.

Page 77.

1.
$$3x^2 - 1 \qquad r = 2x - 2$$
$$x - 0x - 1 \,\overline{\big)\, 3x^4 - 0x^3 - 4x^2 + 2x - 1}$$
$$\underline{-(3x^4 - 0x^3 - 3x^2)}$$
$$0 \quad\quad 0 - x^2 + 2x - 1$$
$$\underline{- (x^2 - 0x + 1)}$$
$$2x - 2$$

2.
$$3x^2 + x - 3 \quad r = -x$$
$$x^2 - x \,\overline{\big)\, 3x^4 - 2x^3 - 4x^2 + 2x}$$
$$\underline{-(3x^4 - 3x^3)}$$
$$x^3 - 4x^2$$
$$\underline{- (x^3 - x^2)}$$
$$-3x^2 + 2x$$
$$\underline{-(-3x^2 + 3x)}$$
$$- x$$

3.
$$x^2 + 1$$
$$x^2 - 2x + 8 \,\overline{\big)\, x^4 - 2x^3 + 9x^2 - 2x + 8}$$
$$\underline{-(x^4 - 2x^3 + 8x^2)}$$
$$0 \quad 0 \quad 1x^2 - 2x + 8$$
$$\underline{-(1x^2 - 2x + 8)}$$
$$0 \quad 0 \quad 0$$

4.
$$2x^2 - 2/3 \qquad r = 4/3x - 53/3$$
$$3x^2 - x - 4 \,\overline{\big)\, 6x^4 - 2x^3 - 10x^2 + \quad 2x - \quad 15}$$
$$\underline{-(6x^4 - 2x^3 - \ 8x^2)}$$
$$0 \quad\quad 0 - 2x^2 + \quad 2x - \quad 15$$
$$\underline{-(- \ 2x^2 + 2/3x^3 + \ 8/3)}$$
$$0 \quad 4/3x - 53/3$$

5.
$$x^2 - 4x - 8 \quad r = 11x + 73$$
$$x^2 - 2x + 6 \,\overline{\big)\, x^4 - 6x^3 + 6x^2 + \ 3x + \ 25}$$
$$\underline{-(x^4 - 2x^3 + 6x^2)}$$
$$0 - 4x^3 + 0x^2 + \ 3x$$
$$\underline{-(- 4x^3 + 8x^2 - 24x)}$$
$$- 8x^2 + 27x + \ 25$$
$$\underline{-(- 8x^2 + 16x - \ 48)}$$
$$11x + \ 73$$

6.

$$
x^2 - x - 4 \overline{\smash{)}\begin{array}{l} -x^2 - 3x - 15 \quad\quad r = -25x - 72 \\ x^4 - 2x^3 - 8x^2 + 2x - 12 \end{array}}
$$

$$
\begin{array}{r}
-x^2 - 3x - 15 \quad\quad r = -25x - 72 \\
x^2 - x - 4 \,\overline{\smash{)}\, x^4 - 2x^3 - 8x^2 + 2x - 12} \\
-(-x^4 + x^3 + 4x^2) \\
\hline
0 - 3x^3 - 12x^2 + 2x \\
-(-3x^3 + 3x^2 + 12x) \\
\hline
0 - 15x^2 - 10x - 12 \\
-(-15x^2 + 15x + 60) \\
\hline
0 - 25x - 72
\end{array}
$$

Page 78.

1.

$$
\begin{array}{r}
3x^2 - 1 \\
x^2 - 0x - 1 \,\overline{\smash{)}\, 3x^4 - 0x^3 - 4x^2 + 2x - 1} \\
-(3x^4 - 0x^3 - 3x^2) \\
\hline
0 \quad 0 - x^2 + 2x - 1 \\
-(-x^2 - 0x + 1) \\
\hline
2x - 2
\end{array}
$$

$$P(x) = d(x)(3x^2 - 1) + 2x - 2$$

2.

$$
\begin{array}{r}
3x^2 + x - 3 \\
x^2 - x \,\overline{\smash{)}\, 3x^4 - 2x^3 - 4x^2 + 2x} \\
-(3x^4 - 3x^3) \\
\hline
0 \quad x^3 - 4x^2 \\
-(x^3 - x^2) \\
\hline
-3x^2 + 2x \\
-(-3x^2 + 3x) \\
\hline
-x
\end{array}
$$

$$P(x) = d(x)(3x^2 + x - 3) - x$$

3.

$$
\begin{array}{r}
x^2 + 1 \\
x^2 - 2x + 8 \,\overline{\smash{)}\, x^4 - 2x^3 + 9x^2 - 2x + 8} \\
-(x^4 - 2x^3 + 8x^2) \\
\hline
0 \quad 0 + x^2 - 2x + 8 \\
-(x^2 - 2x + 8) \\
\hline
0 \quad 0 \quad 0
\end{array}
$$

$$P(x) = d(x)(x^2 + 1)$$

4.

$$
\begin{array}{r}
2x^2 - 2/3 \\
3x^2 - x - 4 \,\overline{\smash{)}\, 6x^4 - 2x^3 - 10x^2 + 2x - 15} \\
-(6x^4 - 2x^3 - 8x^2) \\
\hline
0 \quad 0 - 2x^2 + 2x - 15 \\
-(-2x^2 - 2/3x + 8/3) \\
\hline
0 \quad 4/3x - 53/3
\end{array}
$$

$$P(x) = d(x)(2x^2 - 2/3) + (4/3x - 53/3)$$

5.

$$
\begin{array}{r}
x^2 - 4x - 8 \\
x^2 - 2x + 6 \,\overline{\smash{)}\, x^4 - 6x^3 + 6x^2 + 3x + 25} \\
-(x^4 - 2x^3 + 6x^2) \\
\hline
0 - 4x^3 + 0x^2 + 3x \\
-(-4x^3 + 8x^2 - 24x) \\
\hline
0 - 8x^2 + 27x + 25 \\
-(-8x^2 + 16x - 48) \\
\hline
0 \quad 11x + 73
\end{array}
$$

$$P(x) = d(x)(x^2 - 4x - 8) + (11x + 73)$$

6.

$$
\begin{array}{r}
-x^2 - 3x - 15 \\
x^2 - x - 4 \,\overline{\smash{)}\, -x^4 - 2x^3 - 8x^2 + 2x - 12} \\
-(-x^4 + x^3 + 4x^2) \\
\hline
0 - 3x^3 - 12x^2 + 2x \\
-(-3x^3 + 3x^2 + 12x) \\
\hline
0 - 15x^2 - 10x - 12 \\
-(-15x^2 + 15x + 60) \\
\hline
0 - 25x - 72
\end{array}
$$

$$P(x) = d(x)(-x^2 - 3x - 15) + (-25x - 72)$$

Page 79.

1.
$$
\begin{array}{r|rrrrr}
3 & 4 & -2 & +6 & -5 & -19 \\
  &   & +12 & +30 & +108 & +309 \\
\hline
  & 4 & +10 & +36 & +103 & +290
\end{array}
$$

$$P(x) = (x - 3)(4x^3 + 10x^2 + 36x + 103) + 290$$

2.
$$
\begin{array}{r|rrrrr}
1 & 1 & -4 & +7 & -2 & -9 \\
  &   & +1 & -3 & +4 & +2 \\
\hline
  & 1 & -3 & +4 & +2 & -7
\end{array}
$$

$$P(x) = (x - 1)(x^3 - 3x^2 + 4x + 2) - 7$$

3.
$$
\begin{array}{r|rrrrr}
-2 & 5 & -1 & +2 & -5 & -1 \\
   &   & -10 & +22 & -48 & +106 \\
\hline
   & 5 & -11 & +24 & -53 & +105
\end{array}
$$

$$P(x) = (x + 2)(5x^3 - 11x^2 + 24x - 53) + 105$$

4.
$$
\begin{array}{r|rrrrr}
-4 & 2 & -3 & +7 & -8 & -11 \\
   &   & -8 & +44 & -204 & +848 \\
\hline
   & 2 & -11 & +51 & -212 & +837
\end{array}
$$

$$P(x) = (x + 4)(2x^3 - 11x^2 + 51x - 212) + 837$$

5.
$$
\begin{array}{r|rrrrr}
-10 & 1 & -2 & +3 & -4 & -5 \\
    &   & -10 & +120 & -1230 & +12340 \\
\hline
    & 1 & -12 & +123 & -1234 & +12335
\end{array}
$$

$$P(x) = (x + 10)(x^3 - 12x^2 + 123x - 1234) + 12335$$

6.
$$
\begin{array}{r|rrrrr}
-1 & 6 & -4 & +2 & -0 & -11 \\
   &   & -6 & +10 & -12 & +12 \\
\hline
   & 6 & -10 & +12 & -12 & +1
\end{array}
$$

$$P(x) = (x + 1)(6x^3 - 10x^2 + 12x - 12) + 1$$

Page 80.

1. $\pm 1, \pm \dfrac{1}{3}$

2. $\pm 1, \pm 3, \pm 9$

3. $\pm 1, \pm \dfrac{1}{3}, \pm \dfrac{5}{3}, \pm 5$

4. $\pm 1, \pm 3, \pm 9, \pm \dfrac{1}{5}, \pm \dfrac{3}{5}, \pm \dfrac{9}{5}$

5. $\pm 1, \pm\dfrac{1}{3}$

$$\begin{array}{r|rrrr} 1| & 3 & -7 & +5 & -1 \\ & & -3 & -4 & +1 \\ \hline & 3 & -4 & +1 & 0 \end{array} \quad \text{root}$$

$$\begin{array}{r|rrrr} -1| & 3 & -7 & +5 & -1 \\ & & -3 & +10 & -15 \\ \hline & 3 & -10 & +15 & -16 \end{array} \quad \begin{array}{l}\text{not a}\\ \text{root}\end{array}$$

$$\begin{array}{r|rrrr} 1/3| & 3 & -7 & +5 & -1 \\ & & 1 & -2 & 1 \\ \hline & 3 & -6 & 3 & 0 \end{array} \quad \text{root}$$

$$\begin{array}{r|rrrr} -1/3| & 3 & -7 & +5 & -1 \\ & & -1 & +8/3 & -2/9 \\ \hline & 3 & -8 & +23/3 & -32/9 \end{array} \quad \begin{array}{l}\text{not a}\\ \text{root}\end{array}$$

Page 81.

1.
$$\begin{array}{r|rrrr} 2| & 2 & -4 & +6 & -24 \\ & & 4 & 0 & 12 \\ \hline & 2 & 0 & 6 & -12 \end{array}$$
$(x-2)$ is not a factor
$P(x) = (x-2)(2x^2+6) - 12$

2.
$$\begin{array}{r|rrrr} 5| & 1 & -4 & +6 & -25 \\ & & 5 & 5 & 55 \\ \hline & 1 & 1 & 11 & 30 \end{array}$$
$(x-5)$ is not a factor
5 is not a root
$P(x) = (x-5)(x^2+x+11) + 30$

3.
$$\begin{array}{r|rrrr} 12| & 1 & -32 & +64 & -2112 \\ & & 12 & -240 & -2112 \\ \hline & 1 & -20 & -176 & 0 \end{array}$$
yes, 12 is a factor
$P(x) = (x-12)(x^2-20x-176)$

Page 83.

1.
$$\begin{array}{r|rrrr} 2| & 1 & -7 & +7 & +6 \\ & & 2 & -10 & -6 \\ \hline & 1 & -5 & -3 & 0 \end{array}$$
$(x^2 - 5x - 3)$
$x = \dfrac{5 \pm \sqrt{25 - 4(1)(-3)}}{2}$
$x = \dfrac{5 \pm \sqrt{37}}{2}$ and 2

2.
$$\begin{array}{r|rrrr} 1| & 3 & +5 & -6 & -2 \\ & & 3 & 8 & 2 \\ \hline & 3 & 8 & +2 & 0 \end{array}$$
$3x^2 + 8x + 2$
$x = \dfrac{-8 \pm \sqrt{64 - 4(3)(2)}}{6}$
$x = \dfrac{-8 \pm \sqrt{64 - 24}}{6}$
$x = \dfrac{-8 \pm \sqrt{40}}{6}$
$x = \dfrac{-8 \pm 2\sqrt{10}}{6}$
$x = \dfrac{-4}{3} \pm \dfrac{\sqrt{10}}{3}$, 1

3.
$$\begin{array}{r|rrrrr} 1| & 1 & +8 & +5 & -8 & -6 \\ & & 1 & 9 & 14 & 6 \\ \hline & 1 & 9 & 14 & 6 & 0 \end{array}$$

$$\begin{array}{r|rrrr} -1| & x^3 & +9x^2 & +14x & +6 \\ & & -1 & -8 & -6 \\ \hline & 1 & 8 & 6 & 0 \end{array}$$
$(x^2 + 8x + 6)$
$x = \dfrac{-8 \pm \sqrt{64 - 4(1)(6)}}{2}$
$x = \dfrac{-8 \pm \sqrt{40}}{2} \qquad x = -4 \pm \sqrt{10}, 1, -1$

Page 84. $\dfrac{1}{2}, \dfrac{1}{2}, -\dfrac{2}{3}, \sqrt{2}, -\sqrt{2}$

Page 86.

1. $(-1 - 3, -6, -4)$
$(-4, -10)$
$|u| = r = \sqrt{(-4)^2 + (10)^2}$
$\quad = \sqrt{116}$
$\quad = 10.77$
$\theta = -\cos^{-1}\left(\dfrac{-4}{10.77}\right)$
$\theta = -111.8°$
$(10.77, -111.8)$

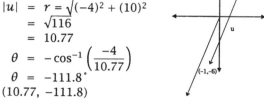

2. $(3 - (2), 5 - (-11))$
$(5, 6)$
$r = |4| = \sqrt{25 + 36}$
$\quad = \sqrt{61}$
$\theta = \cos^{-1}\left(\dfrac{5}{\sqrt{61}}\right)$
$\theta = 50.2°$
$(\sqrt{61}, 50.2°)$

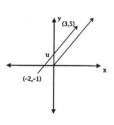

3. $(-2(-2), 1 - 4)$
$(-4, -3)$
$r = |u| = \sqrt{16 + 9}$
$r = 5$
$\theta = -\cos^{-1}\left(\dfrac{-4}{5}\right)$
$\theta = -143.13°$
$(5, 143.13°)$

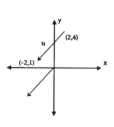

4. $(4 - (-4), -3 - (-6))$
$(8, 3)$
$r = |u| = \sqrt{64 + 9}$
$r = \sqrt{73}$
$\theta = \cos^{-1}\left(\dfrac{8}{\sqrt{73}}\right)$
$\theta = 20.56°$
$(\sqrt{73}, 20.56°)$

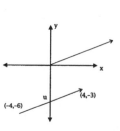

Page 87.

1. $u \cdot v = 4(-8) + -4(10) = -72$
not perpendicular

2. $u \cdot v = 7(24) + -12(14) = 168 - 168 = 0$
    perpendicular

3. $u \cdot v = 27(2) + 32(-3) = 59 - 96 = -42$
    not perpendicular

4. $u \cdot v = 6(3) + -4(-2) = 26$
    not perpendicular
    but coincidental

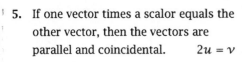

5. If one vector times a scalor equals the
    other vector, then the vectors are
    parallel and coincidental. $2u = v$

Page 88.

1. $u \cdot v = 6(-2) + -3(-5) = 3$
    $|u| = \sqrt{45}$
    $|v| = \sqrt{29}$
    $\theta = \cos^{-1}\left(\dfrac{3}{\sqrt{45} \cdot \sqrt{29}}\right)$
    $\theta = 85.2°$

2. $u \cdot v = -3(-4) + (-10)(4) = -28$
    $|u| = \sqrt{109}$
    $|v| = 4\sqrt{2}$
    $\theta = \cos^{-1}\left(\dfrac{-28}{\sqrt{109} \cdot 4\sqrt{2}}\right)$
    $\theta = 118.3°$

3. $u \cdot v = 9(1) + (-8)(-5) = -31$
    $|u| = \sqrt{145}$
    $|v| = \sqrt{26}$
    $\theta = \cos^{-1}\left(\dfrac{-31}{\sqrt{145} \cdot \sqrt{26}}\right)$
    $\theta = 120.3°$

4. $u \cdot v = 7(-5) + 12(5) = 25$
    $|u| = \sqrt{193}$
    $|v| = 5\sqrt{2}$
    $\theta = \cos^{-1}\left(\dfrac{25}{\sqrt{193} \cdot 5\sqrt{2}}\right)$
    $\theta = 75.3°$

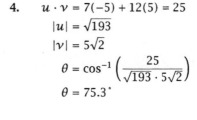

Page 89.

1. $f(4) = -(4)^2 + 4 = -12$
    $f(0) = -(0)^2 + 4 = +4$
    $\dfrac{-12 - 4}{4 - 0} = -4$ -4 is the average rate of change

2. $f(5) = \dfrac{2}{5}$
    $f(i) = \dfrac{2}{1}$
    $\dfrac{\frac{2}{5} - 2}{5 - 1} = \dfrac{\frac{-8}{5}}{4} = \dfrac{-8}{5} \cdot \dfrac{1}{4} = \dfrac{-2}{5}$

3. $f(2) = (2)^4 - 3(2)^2 + 4 = 8$
    $f(1) = (-1)^4 - 3(-1)^2 + 4 = 2$
    $\dfrac{8 - 2}{2 - (-1)} = \dfrac{6}{3} = 2$

1. $v(4) = 6(4)^2 + 3(4) = 108$
    $v(1) = 6(1)^2 + 3(1) = 9$
    $\dfrac{108 - 9}{4 - 1} = \dfrac{99}{3} = 33$

2. $v(10) = 4.9(10)^2 + 1.6(10) + 10 = 516$
    $v(1) = 4.9(1)^2 + 1.6(1) + 10 = 16.5$
    $\dfrac{516 - 16.5}{10 - 1} = \dfrac{499.5}{9} = 55.5$

Page 91.

1. $f(x + h) = (x + h)^3 - 4$
    $f'(x) = \lim_{h \to 0} (x + h)^3 - 4 - (x^3 - 4)$
    $f'(x) = \lim_{h \to 0} \dfrac{(x^3 + 3x^2h + 3xh^2 + h^3) - 4 - x^3 + 4}{h}$
    $f'(x) = \lim_{h \to 0} \dfrac{(3x^2h + +3xh^2 + h^3)}{h} = \lim_{h \to 0} \dfrac{h(3x^2 + 3xh + h^2)}{h} = 3x^2$

2. $f(x + h) = 3(x + h)^3 - 4(x + h) + 5$

$f'(x) = \lim_{h \to 0} 3(x + h)^3 - 4(x + h) + 5 - (3x^3 - 4x + 5)$

$f'(x) = \lim_{h \to 0} \dfrac{3x^3 + 9x^2h + 9xh^2 + 3h^3 - 4x - 4h + 5 - 3x^3 + 4x - 5}{h}$

$f'(x) = \lim_{h \to 0} \dfrac{9x^2h + 9xh^2 + 3h^3 - 4h}{h} = \lim_{h \to 0} \dfrac{h(9x^2 + 9xh + 3h^2 - 4)}{h} = 9x^2 - 4$

3. $f(x + h) = 3(x + h)^2 - (x + h) + 27$

$f'(x) = \lim_{h \to 0} \dfrac{3(x + h)^2 - (x + h) + 27 - (3x^2 - x + 27)}{h}$

$f'(x) = \lim_{h \to 0} \dfrac{3x^2 + 6xh + 3h^2 - x - h + 27 - 3x^2 - x - 27}{h} = \lim_{h \to 0} \dfrac{h(6x + 3h - 1)}{h} = 6x - 1$

4. $f(x + h) = (x + h)^4 + 2(x + h)^2 - 8$

$f'(x) = \lim_{h \to 0} \dfrac{x^4 + 4x^3h + 6x^2h^2 + 4xh^3 + h^4 + 2(x^2 + 2xh + h^2) - 8 - (x^4 + 2x^2 - 8)}{h}$

$f'(x) = \lim_{h \to 0} \dfrac{x^4 + 4x^3h + 6x^2h^2 + 4xh^3 + h^4 + 2x^2 + 4xh + 2h^2 - 8 - x^4 - 2x^2 + 8}{h}$

$f'(x) = \lim_{h \to 0} \dfrac{h(4x^3 + 6x^2h + 4xh^2 + h^3 + 4x + 2h)}{h} = 4x^3 + 4x$

Page 92.

1. $f(1 + h) = (1 + h)^3 - (1 + h)$

$f'(1) = \lim_{h \to 0} \dfrac{(1 + h)^3 - (1 + h) - (1^3 - 1)}{h}$

$f'(1) = \lim_{h \to 0} \dfrac{1 + 3h + 3h^2 + h^3 - 1 - h}{h}$

$f'(1) = \lim_{h \to 0} \dfrac{h(2 + 3h + h^2)}{h} = 2$

2. $f(-7 + h) = 2(-7 + h)^2 - 3(-7 + h)$

$\qquad = +98 - 28h + 2h^2 + 21 - 3h$

$\qquad = 119 - 31h + 2h^2$

$f'(-7) = \lim_{h \to 0} \dfrac{119 - 31h + 2h^2 - 119}{h}$

$f'(-7) = \lim_{h \to 0} \dfrac{-31h + 2h^2}{h}$

$f'(-7) = \lim_{h \to 0} \dfrac{h(-31 + 2h)}{h} = -31$

Page 93.

1. $f(2 + \triangle t) = 3(2 + \triangle t)^2 - 4(2 + \triangle t) + 8$

$f(2 + \triangle t) = 12 + 12\triangle t + 3(\triangle t)^2 - 8 - 4\triangle t + 8$

$f(2 + \triangle t) = 12 + 8\triangle t + 3\triangle t^2$

$f'(2) = \lim_{\triangle t \to 0} \dfrac{12 + 8\triangle t + 3\triangle t^2 - 12}{\triangle t}$

$f'(2) = \lim_{\triangle t \to 0} \dfrac{\triangle t(8 + 3\triangle t)}{\triangle t} = 8$

2. $f(3 + \triangle t) = 4.9(3 + \triangle t)^2 + 16(3 + \triangle t) + 10$

$f(3 + \triangle t) = 44.1 + 29.4\triangle t + 4.9(\triangle t)^2 + 48 + 16t + 10$

$f(3 + \triangle t) = 102.1 + 45.4\triangle t + 4.9(\triangle t)^2$

$f'(3) = \lim_{\triangle t \to 0} \dfrac{102.1 + 45.4\triangle t + 4.9(\triangle t)^2 - 102.1}{\triangle t}$

$f'(3) = \lim_{\triangle t \to 0} \dfrac{\triangle t(45.4 + 4.9\triangle t)}{\triangle t} = 45.4$

3. $f(10 - \triangle t) = 5(10 - \triangle t)^2 - 4$

$\qquad = 500 - 100\triangle t - 5(\triangle t)^2 - 4$

$\qquad = 496 - 100\triangle t - 5(\triangle t)^2$

$f'(10) = \lim_{\triangle t \to 0} \dfrac{496 - 100\triangle t - 5(\triangle t)^2 - 496}{\triangle t}$

$f'(10) = \lim_{\triangle t \to 0} \dfrac{\triangle t(-100 - 5\triangle t)}{\triangle t} = 100$

4. $f(3 + \triangle t) = (3 + \triangle t)^3 - 3(3 + 3\triangle t)^2 - 1$

$f(3 + \triangle t) = 27 + 27\triangle t + 9\triangle t^2 + (\triangle t)^3$

$f(3 + \triangle t) = -1 + 9\triangle t + 6(\triangle t)^2 + (\triangle t)^3$

$f'(3) = \lim\limits_{\triangle t \to 0} \dfrac{-1 + 9\triangle t + 6(\triangle t)^2 + (\triangle t)^3 + 1}{\triangle t}$

$f'(3) = \lim\limits_{\triangle t \to 0} \dfrac{\triangle t(+9\triangle t + 6\triangle t + (\triangle t)^2)}{\triangle t} = 9$

Page 95.

1. $f(x + h) = (x + h + 3)^{\frac{1}{2}}$

$f'(x) = \lim\limits_{h \to 0} \dfrac{(x + h + 3)^{\frac{1}{2}} - (x + 3)^{\frac{1}{2}}}{h} \cdot \dfrac{(x + h + 3)^{\frac{1}{2}} + (x + 3)^{\frac{1}{2}}}{(x + h + 3)^{\frac{1}{2}} + (x + 3)^{\frac{1}{2}}}$

$f'(x) = \lim\limits_{h \to 0} \dfrac{(x + h + 3) - (x + 3)^{\frac{1}{2}}(x + h + 3)^{\frac{1}{2}} + (x + 3)^{\frac{1}{2}}(x + h + 3)^{\frac{1}{2}} - (x + 3)}{h[(x + h + 3)^{\frac{1}{2}} + (x + 3)^{\frac{1}{2}}]}$

$f'(x) = \lim\limits_{h \to 0} \dfrac{x + h + 3 - x - 3}{h[(x + h + 3)^{\frac{1}{2}} + (x + 3)^{\frac{1}{2}}]} = \lim\limits_{h \to 0} \dfrac{1}{(x + h + 3)^{\frac{1}{2}} + (x + 3)^{\frac{1}{2}}} = \dfrac{1}{2(x + 3)^{\frac{1}{2}}}$

2. $f(x + h) = (2 - 3(x + h))^{\frac{1}{2}}$

$f'(x) = \lim\limits_{h \to 0} \dfrac{(2 - 3x - 3h)^{\frac{1}{2}}}{h} \cdot \dfrac{(2 - 3x - 3h)^{\frac{1}{2}} + (2 - 3x)^{\frac{1}{2}}}{(2 - 3x - 3h)^{\frac{1}{2}} + (2 - 3x)^{\frac{1}{2}}}$

$f'(x) = \lim\limits_{h \to 0} \dfrac{2 - 3x - 3h - (2 - 3x)^{\frac{1}{2}}(2 - 3x - 3h)^{\frac{1}{2}} + (2 - 3x)^{\frac{1}{2}}(2 - 3x - 3h)^{\frac{1}{2}} - (2 - 3x)}{h[(2 - 3x - 3h)^{\frac{1}{2}} + (2 - 3x)^{\frac{1}{2}}]}$

$f'(x) = \lim\limits_{h \to 0} \dfrac{2 - 3x - 3h - 2 + 3x}{h[(2 - 3x - 3h)^{\frac{1}{2}} + (2 - 3x)^{\frac{1}{2}}]} = \lim\limits_{h \to 0} \dfrac{-3}{(2 - 3x - 3h)^{\frac{1}{2}} + (2 - 3x)^{\frac{1}{2}}} = \dfrac{-3}{2(2 - 3x)^{\frac{1}{2}}}$

3. $f(x + h) = 3(x + h - 2)^{\frac{1}{2}}$

$f'(x) = \lim\limits_{h \to 0} \dfrac{3(x + h - 2)^{\frac{1}{2}} - 3(x - 2)^{\frac{1}{2}}}{h} \cdot \dfrac{3(x + h - 2)^{\frac{1}{2}} + 3(x - 2)^{\frac{1}{2}}}{3(x + h - 2)^{\frac{1}{2}} + 3(x - 2)^{\frac{1}{2}}}$

$f'(x) = \lim\limits_{h \to 0} \dfrac{9(x + h - 2) - 9(x - 2)^{\frac{1}{2}}(x + h - 2)^{\frac{1}{2}} + 9(x - 2)^{\frac{1}{2}}(x + h - 2)^{\frac{1}{2}} - 9(x - 2)}{h[3(x + h - 2)^{\frac{1}{2}} + 3(x - 2)^{\frac{1}{2}}]}$

$f'(x) = \lim\limits_{h \to 0} \dfrac{9x + 9h - 18 - 9x + 18}{h[3(x + h - 2)^{\frac{1}{2}} + 3(x - 2)^{\frac{1}{2}}]} = \lim\limits_{h \to 0} \dfrac{9}{3(x + h - 2)^{\frac{1}{2}} + 3(x - 2)^{\frac{1}{2}}} = \dfrac{9}{6(x - 2)^{\frac{1}{2}}} = \dfrac{3}{2(x - 2)^{\frac{1}{2}}}$

4. $f(x + h) = 2(1 - x - h)^{\frac{1}{2}}$

$f'(x) = \lim\limits_{h \to 0} \dfrac{2(1 - x - h)^{\frac{1}{2}} - 2(1 - x)^{\frac{1}{2}}}{h} \cdot \dfrac{2(1 - x - h)^{\frac{1}{2}} + 2(1 - x)^{\frac{1}{2}}}{2(1 - x - h)^{\frac{1}{2}} + 2(1 - x)^{\frac{1}{2}}}$

$f'(x) = \lim\limits_{h \to 0} \dfrac{4(1 - x - h) - 2(1 - x)^{\frac{1}{2}}2(1 - x - h)^{\frac{1}{2}} + 2(1 - x)^{\frac{1}{2}}2(1 - x - h)^{\frac{1}{2}} - 4(1 - x)}{h[2(1 - x - h)^{\frac{1}{2}} + 2(1 - x)^{\frac{1}{2}}]}$

$f'(x) = \lim\limits_{h \to 0} \dfrac{4 - 4x - 4h - 4 + 4x}{h[2(1 - x - h)^{\frac{1}{2}} + 2(1 - x)^{\frac{1}{2}}]} = \lim\limits_{h \to 0} \dfrac{-4}{2(1 - x - h)^{\frac{1}{2}} + 2(1 - x)^{\frac{1}{2}}} = \dfrac{-4}{4(1 - x)^{\frac{1}{2}}} = \dfrac{-1}{(1 - x)^{\frac{1}{2}}}$

Page 97.

1. $f(x + h) = \dfrac{3}{2(x + h) - 3}$

$f'(x) = \lim\limits_{h \to 0} \dfrac{\frac{3}{2(x+h)-3} - \frac{3}{2x-3}}{h} = \lim\limits_{h \to 0} \dfrac{3(2x - 3) - [3(2(x+h) - 3)]}{\frac{[2(x+h)-3](2x-3)}{h}} = \lim\limits_{h \to 0} \dfrac{6x - 9 - 6x - 6h + 9}{[2(x+h) - 3](2x - 3)} \cdot \dfrac{1}{h}$

$f'(x) = \lim\limits_{h \to 0} \dfrac{-6}{[(2(x+h) - 3)](2x - 3)} = \dfrac{-6}{(2x - 3)^2} = f'(3) \dfrac{-6}{(2(4) - 3)^2} = \dfrac{-6}{25}$

2. $f(x + h) = \dfrac{-1}{4 - 3(x + h)}$

$f'(x) = \lim\limits_{h \to 0} \dfrac{\frac{-1}{4-3(x+h)} - \frac{-1}{4-3x}}{h} = \lim\limits_{h \to 0} \dfrac{\frac{-1(4-3x)+1(4-3x-3h)}{(4-3(x+h))(4-3x)}}{h} = \lim\limits_{h \to 0} \dfrac{-4 + 3x + 4 - 3x - 3h}{(4 - 3(x + h))(4 - 3x)} \cdot \dfrac{1}{h}$

$f'(x) = \lim\limits_{h \to 0} \dfrac{-3}{(4 - 3(x + h))(4 - 3x)} = \dfrac{-3}{(4 - 3x)^2} = f'(-2) = \dfrac{-3}{(4 - 3(-2))^2} = \dfrac{-3}{100}$

3. $f(x + h) = \dfrac{10}{2(x + h) - 6}$

$f'(x) = \lim\limits_{h \to 0} \dfrac{\frac{10}{2(x+h)-6} - \frac{10}{2x-6}}{h} = \lim\limits_{h \to 0} \dfrac{10(2x - 6) - 10(2(x + h) - 6)}{(2(x + h) - 6)(2x - 6)} \cdot \dfrac{1}{h}$

$f'(x) = \lim\limits_{h \to 0} \dfrac{20x - 60 - 20x + 60}{(2(x + h) - 6)(2x - 6)h} = \lim\limits_{h \to 0} \dfrac{-20}{(2(x + h) - 6)(2x - 6)} = \dfrac{-20}{(2x - 6)^2} = f'(5) = \dfrac{20}{(2(50) - 6)^2} = \dfrac{-20}{16} = \dfrac{-5}{4}$

4. $f(x + h) = \dfrac{3}{x + h - 5}$

$f'(x) = \lim\limits_{h \to 0} \dfrac{\frac{3}{x+h-5} - \frac{3}{x-5}}{h} = \lim\limits_{h \to 0} \dfrac{3(x - 5) - 3(x + h - 5)}{(x + h - 5)(x - 5)} \cdot \dfrac{1}{h} = \lim\limits_{h \to 0} \dfrac{3x - 15 - 5x - 3h + 15}{(x + h - 5)(x - 5)} \cdot \dfrac{1}{h}$

$f'(x) = \lim\limits_{h \to 0} \dfrac{-3}{(x + h - 5)(x - 5)} = \dfrac{-3}{(x - 5)^2} = f'(1) = \dfrac{-3}{(1 - 5)^2} = \dfrac{-3}{16}$

Page 99.

1. $f(x) = 3x^2 - 2$ is a quadratic formula. $a = 3$ $b = 0$

$f'(x) = 2(3)x + 0 = 6x$

$f'(1) = 6$

$f(1) = 1$

$m = 6 \ (1, 1)$ $y - 1 = 6(x - 1)$

2. $f(x + h) = \dfrac{2}{x + h}$

$f'(x) = \lim\limits_{h \to 0} \dfrac{\frac{2}{x+2} - \frac{2}{x}}{h} = \lim\limits_{h \to 0} \dfrac{2x - 2x - 2h}{(x + h)(x)} \cdot \dfrac{1}{h}$

$= \dfrac{-2}{x^2} = f'(4) = \dfrac{-2}{4^2} = \dfrac{-1}{8}$

$m = \dfrac{-1}{8}$ $f(4) = \dfrac{1}{2}$ $\left(4, \dfrac{1}{2}\right)$

$y - \dfrac{1}{8} = \dfrac{-1}{8}(x - 4)$

3. $f(x + h) = (x + h)^{\frac{1}{2}}$

$f'(x) = \lim\limits_{h \to 0} \dfrac{(x + h)^{\frac{1}{2}} - x^{\frac{1}{2}}}{h} \cdot \dfrac{(x + h)^{\frac{1}{2}} + x^{\frac{1}{2}}}{(x + h)^{\frac{1}{2}} + x^{\frac{1}{2}}}$

$= \lim\limits_{h \to 0} \dfrac{x + h - x}{[(x + h)^{\frac{1}{2}} + x^{\frac{1}{2}}]} = \dfrac{1}{2x^{\frac{1}{2}}}$

$f'(9) = \dfrac{1}{6}$ $m = \dfrac{1}{6}$ $f(9) = 3$ $(9, 3)$

$y = -3 = \dfrac{1}{6}(x - 9)$

4. $f(x + h) = 4(x + h)^4$

$f'(x) = \lim\limits_{h \to 0} \dfrac{4x^4 + 16x^3h + 24x^2h^2 + 16xh^3 + 4x^2 - 4x^4}{h}$

$= \lim\limits_{h \to 0} \dfrac{h(16x^3 + 24x^2h + 16xh^2 + 4h^3)}{h}$

$f'(x) = 16x^3$ $f'(-2) = -128$ $f(-2) = 64$

$m = -128$ $(-2, 64)$ $y - 64 = -128(x + 2)$

Page 100.

1. $f'(x) = 6x - 2$
2. $f'(x) = 49x^6 - 9x^2$
3. $f'(x) = 2 - 6x - 16x^3 + 7$
4. $f'(x) = -2x^{-3} + 2x$
5. $f'(x) = 4x - 3 - 2x^{-2}$
6. $f'(x) = \dfrac{-2}{(2x)^2}$
7. $f'(x) = 40x^3 - 4x$
8. $f'(x) = -19.6x + 160$

Page 102.

1. $3x^3 - 12x^2 + 12x - 3$
   $9x^2 - 24x + 12$
   $3(3x^2 - 8x + 4)$
   $3(3x - 2)(x - 2)$
   $\dfrac{2}{3}, 2$

   Increasing when $x < \dfrac{2}{3}$ and $x > 2$

   Decreasing when $\dfrac{2}{3} < x < 2$

   $y = .55 \quad y = -3$

2. $3x^2 - 6x - 45$
   $3(x^2 - 2x - 15)$
   $3(x + 3)(x - 5)$
   $-3, 5$
   Increasing when $x < -3$ and $x > 5$
   Decreasing when $-3 < x < 5$
   $y = 136 \quad y = -174$

3. $6x^2 - 78x + 72$
   $6(x^2 - 13x + 12)$
   $(x - 12)(x - 1)$
   1, 12
   Increasing when $x < 1$ and $x > 12$
   Decreasing when $1 < x < 12$
   $y = 31 \quad y = -1300$

Page 103.

1. $f'(x) = 0$ at $x = 0$, $x = 5$
   $f'(x) > 0$ when $x < 0$, $x > 5$
   $f'(x) < 0$ when $0 < x < 5$

2. $f'(x) = 9x^2 - 27 = 0$
   $= 9(x^2 - 3) = 0$
   $x = \sqrt{3} \quad x = -\sqrt{3}$
   (where horizontal tangents occur)
   $f(x)$ increasing when $x < -\sqrt{3}$ and $x > \sqrt{3}$
   $P(x)$ decreasing when $-\sqrt{3} < x < \sqrt{3}$

3. $\begin{array}{r|rrrr} 1 & 4 & 3 & -90 & +83 \\ & & 4 & 7 & -83 \\ \hline & 4 & 7 & -83 & 0 \end{array}$
   $4x^2 + 7x - 83 = 0$
   $x = \dfrac{-7 \pm \sqrt{49 + 16 - 83}}{8}$
   zeros: $x = 1$, $x = 3.76$ and $x = -5.51$
   $f'(x) = 12x^2 + 6x - 90 = 0$
   $= 6(2x^2 + x - 15) = 0$
   $= 6(2x - 5)(x + 3) = 0$
   $x = \dfrac{5}{2} \quad x = -3$

   $f(x)$ increasing when $x < -3$ and $x > \dfrac{5}{2}$

   $f(x)$ decreasing when $-3 < x < \dfrac{5}{2}$

   $f'(2) = -30 \quad m = -30$
   $f(2) = -53 \quad (2, -53)$
   $y + 53 = -30(x - 2)$

Page 104.

1. $(x + h)^3 = x^3 + 3x^2h + 3xh^2 + h^3$

2. $f'(x) = \lim\limits_{h \to 0} \dfrac{x^3 + 3x^2h + 3xh^2 + h^3 - 2(x + h) + 4 - (x^3 - 2x + 4)}{h}$

   $f'(x) = \lim\limits_{h \to 0} \dfrac{x^3 + 3x^2h + 3xh^2 + h^3 - 2x - 2h + 4 - x^3 + 2x - 4}{h}$

   $f'(x) = \lim\limits_{h \to 0} \dfrac{h(3x^2 + 3xh + h^2 - 2)}{h} = 3x^2 - 2$

3a. $f'(x) = 16x - 2$

3b. $f(-2) = 16(-2) - 2 = -34$

4a. $v(t) = -6t + 5$
    $a(t) = -6$

4b. $v(5) = -25$
    $a(5) = -6$

Page 105.

1. $f(12) = 418 \qquad f(3) = 31$

   $\dfrac{418 - 31}{12 - 3} = \dfrac{387}{9} = 43$

2. $f(-2) = \dfrac{-1}{2} \qquad f(-10) = \dfrac{-1}{10}$

   $\dfrac{\frac{1}{2} + \frac{1}{10}}{-2 - (-10)} = \dfrac{-4}{10} \cdot \dfrac{1}{8} = \dfrac{1}{20}$

3. $f\left(\dfrac{5\pi}{6}\right) = \sin\dfrac{10\pi}{6} = \sin\dfrac{5\pi}{3} = \dfrac{-\sqrt{3}}{2}$

   $\dfrac{\frac{-\sqrt{3}}{2} - 0}{\frac{5\pi}{6} - \frac{\pi}{2}} = \dfrac{\frac{-\sqrt{3}}{2}}{\frac{\pi}{3}} = \dfrac{-3\sqrt{3}}{2\pi}$

   $f\left(\dfrac{\pi}{2}\right) = \sin 2\left(\dfrac{\pi}{2}\right) = \sin\pi = 0$

4. $f(6) = -61 \qquad f(2) = -9$

   $\dfrac{-61 + 9}{6 - 2} = \dfrac{-52}{4} = -13$

5. $f(x) = \dfrac{2}{3}x^{-1} \qquad f'(x) - \dfrac{-2}{3}x^{-2}$

6. $f'(2) = \dfrac{-2}{3}(2)^{-2} = \dfrac{-2}{3.4} = \dfrac{-2}{12} = \dfrac{-1}{6}$

Page 106.

- $\begin{array}{r|rrrr} 1] & 4 + 4 & - 32 & + 24 \\ & 4 & 8 & - 24 \\ \hline & 4 \quad 8 & - 24 & \quad 0 \end{array}$

  $4x^2 + 8x - 24 = 0$

  $x^2 + 2x - 6 = 0$

  $x = \dfrac{-2 \pm \sqrt{28}}{2}$

  $= -2 \pm 2\sqrt{7}$

  $= -1 \pm \sqrt{7}$

- $1, -1 - \sqrt{7}, -1 + \sqrt{7}$
- $y = 24$
- $12x^2 + 8x - 32$
- $y = 72 \qquad y = -2.07$
- $x < -2x > \dfrac{4}{3}$
- $-2 < x < \dfrac{4}{3}$
- $(x - 1)(x - (-1 - \sqrt{7}))(x - (-1 + \sqrt{7}))$
- $y - 464 = 308(x - 5)$
- $-1 - \sqrt{7} < x < 1$ and $x > -1 + \sqrt{7}$
- $x < -1 - \sqrt{7}$ and $1 < x < -1 + \sqrt{7}$